CREATIVE SILVER CHAINS

CREATIVE SILVER CHAINS
20 DAZZLING DESIGNS

CHANTAL LISE SAUNDERS

LARK BOOKS

A Division of Sterling Publishing Co., Inc.
New York

Editor: **Suzanne J. E. Tourtillott**
Art Director: **Kathleen Holmes**
Cover Designer: **Barbara Zaretsky**
Photographer: **Stewart O'Shields**
Associate Editor: **Nathalie Mornu**
Associate Art Director: **Shannon Yokeley**
Editorial Assistance: **Delores Gosnell**
Editorial Interns: **Kelly J. Johnson and Metta L. Pry**
Photo on page 8 courtesy of Handy & Harman/Lucas-Milhaupt, Inc.

Library of Congress Cataloging-in-Publication Data
Saunders, Chantal Lise.
    Creative silver chains : 20 dazzling designs / Chantal Lise Saunders.—1st ed.
        p.   cm.
    Includes index.
    ISBN 1-57990-615-X (hardcover)
    1. Jewelry making.   2. Chains (Jewelry)   3. Silver jewelry—Technique.   I. Title.
TT212.S28 2005
739.27—dc22

                            2005004467

10 9 8 7 6 5 4 3 2

First Edition

Published by Lark Books, A Division of Sterling Publishing Co., Inc., 387 Park Avenue
South, New York, N.Y. 10016

Text and project designs © 2005, Chantal Lise Saunders
Photography © 2005, Lark Books

Distributed in Canada by Sterling Publishing c/o Canadian Manda Group, 165 Dufferin
Street, Toronto, Ontario, Canada M6K 3H6

Distributed in the U.K. by Guild of Master Craftsman Publications Ltd., Castle Place, 166
High Street, Lewes, East Sussex, England BN7 1XU Tel: (+ 44) 1273 477374, Fax: (+ 44)
1273 478606, e-mail: pubs@thegmcgroup.com, Web: www.gmcpublications.com

Distributed in Australia by Capricorn Link (Australia) Pty Ltd., P.O. Box 704, Windsor,
NSW 2756 Australia

If you have questions or comments about this book, please contact:
Lark Books
67 Broadway
Asheville, NC 28801
(828) 253-0467

Manufactured in China

ISBN 1-57990-615-x

For information about custom editions, special sales, premiums, and corporate purchases,
please contact Sterling Special Sales Department at 800-805-5489 or
specialsales@sterlingpub.com.

Contents

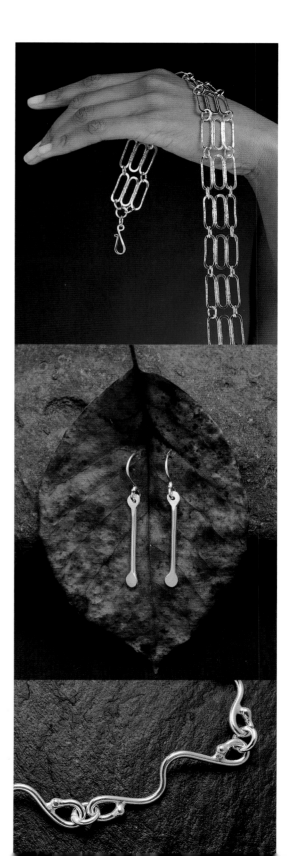

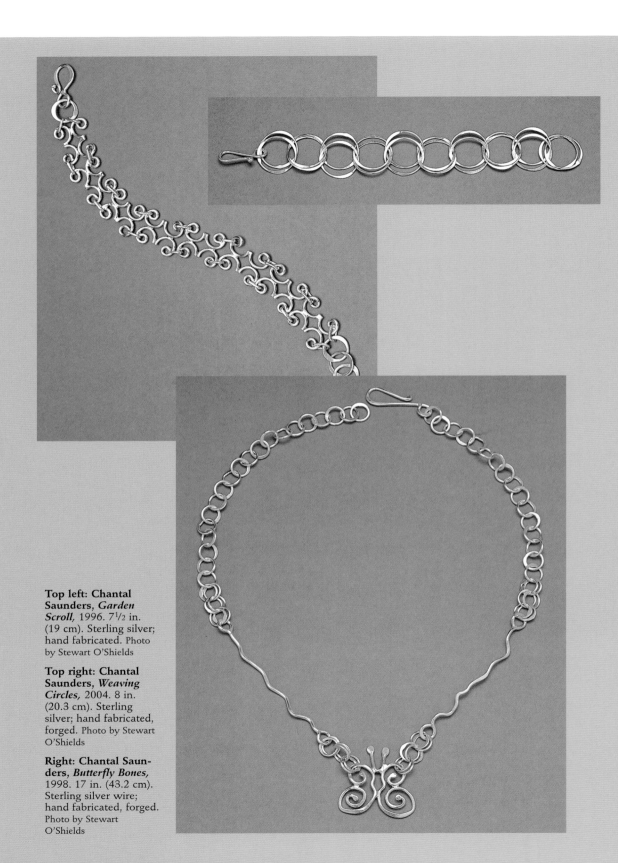

Top left: Chantal Saunders, *Garden Scroll,* 1996. 7¹/₂ in. (19 cm). Sterling silver; hand fabricated. Photo by Stewart O'Shields

Top right: Chantal Saunders, *Weaving Circles,* 2004. 8 in. (20.3 cm). Sterling silver; hand fabricated, forged. Photo by Stewart O'Shields

Right: Chantal Saunders, *Butterfly Bones,* 1998. 17 in. (43.2 cm). Sterling silver wire; hand fabricated, forged. Photo by Stewart O'Shields

Artful Chain Making

WE WEAR CHAINS CLOSE to the body. They carry the mementos of life and showcase hand, wrist, and face. Links gently shift, creating tinkling sounds. Light shines and glistens from metal that is hard and durable yet elegant and delicate. Chains can be sexy or strong, making us feel that way, too. And when you make them yourself, chains can be lifelong expressions of your soul.

Wire is a remarkable metal form, as vital to modern chain making as it was to the ancients. Gold wire was used in Egypt as early as 3000 B.C.E., and led, naturally enough, to the idea of making wire rings. These were surely inspired by the shapes of fingers, necks, and wrists. In fact, metal chains were an early art form in most cultures. As far back as 4,000 years ago, chain-mail body armor was made from many thousands of tiny metal rings joined into a fabric-like mesh. Today, chains and their applications continue to be both utilitarian and decorative. Many of the 200 or so styles of chain found around the world today remain unchanged since they were devised centuries ago. Once worn only by royalty, precious metal chains are now commonplace.

Modern chain making has been delegated mostly to machines, with an inevitable loss of originality and quality. You'll be glad to know that making sterling silver chain by hand is surprisingly easy to learn. Simple hand tools bring this jeweler's art back to the most essential and elementary techniques of working with wire. In this book I'll show you how to make what are sometimes referred to as "fancy chains" that no one could ever mistake as machine made. The design of these artful chains often begins with a simple circle as a basic unit, or link. Joined together, handcrafted links become spirited, artistic pieces in their own right.

I wrote this book to share with you how I make my unique silver chains. After you have gathered the necessary tools and materials described in Studio Essentials, I show you how to handle them in the Techniques section. I demonstrate how to move the wire in basic ways, and how to most effectively use the tools and your hands to do so. For beginners, there are special warm-up exercises. Finally, the chain-making concepts described in the Design chapter should provide a good foundation for your creative imagination. The first few step-by-step projects are easy ones that will help you put your basic skills to satisfying use. If you're new to wire work, I suggest that you try the projects in the order (more or less) they're given, because the latter ones are definitely more challenging.

Over the years, people have often suggested that I use casting to speed up my production, but exactly identical links result in a design that can seem stiff or machine made. Handmade links are only similar, never identical. Handmade chains can express fluid movements of shape and light, and give expression to the power of chance in creating art. I hope that the techniques and designs shown here will inspire you to make your own artful chains.

Materials

Pure silver is a white metal that's generally too soft for chain applications. Mixing copper with silver creates the alloy known as sterling silver, which has just the right amount of strength and malleability to make it a popular jeweler's metal.

Sterling silver is a beautiful material to work with. It's a versatile, durable, affordable metal, malleable enough to bend by hand, and quite forgiving of the beginning chain maker. Certainly in your own studio you could use gold, platinum, copper, brass, and even steel.

In the United States, wire sold as "sterling silver" contains a standard ratio of 92.5 parts of silver to 7.5 parts of copper. You can purchase coils or spools of various gauges of sterling silver wire from a refiner or a jewelry supplier; cost is determined by the day's market price per troy ounce. One drawback is sterling's tendency to tarnish, because airborne sulfur causes the copper to oxidize, leaving a gray film of cupric oxide on the metal's surface. Store your raw materials and jewelry in airtight containers and tarnish will rarely be a problem.

All the chains in this book are made with sterling silver wire. The thickness of a wire is measured by its gauge, or diameter. A thinner wire is indicated with an increase in the gauge number. The thickest sterling silver wire available is gauge 4, which is about .204 inch (5.18 mm) thick. Thinner wires aren't strong enough to be used alone, and thicker wire is "cold," or harder to shape by hand at room temperature. See the chart on page 106 for a list of wire gauges and their equivalent diameters.

A good jewelry supplier's catalog can be very informative but also a little overwhelming; there are so many kinds, styles, and sizes of silver wire. Each kind has special working characteristics, so be sure to use *dead soft* round sterling silver. Dead soft means that the metal has been *annealed*, or heated, until its molecular structure is relaxed and soft. When silver is formed

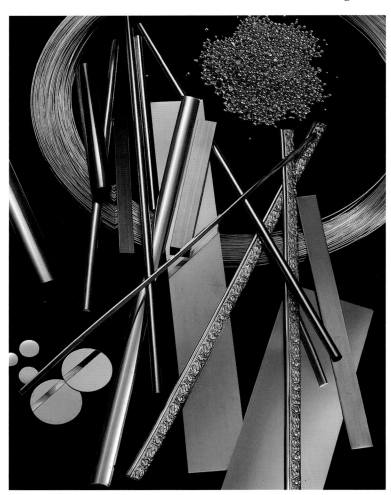

Silver comes in many forms.

into wire, it becomes work hardened, or brittle and rigid. You'll need 20-, 18-, 16-, and 14-gauge wires, which are sold in coils and priced by the troy ounce. The chart below shows how much length you can expect from an ounce of sterling silver wire.

Sterling Silver 1-Ounce (28 g)/Length Equivalents

20 gauge	18 gauge	16 gauge	14 gauge
228 inches (5.9 m)	144 inches (3.7 m)	90 inches (2.3 m)	55 inches (1.4 m)

The round style is best to start with, though square, half round, and even triangular wires are available. You might find half-hard sterling silver wire, but it's not worth purchasing if you intend to do any soldering, because you'll anneal the wire in the process.

The projects in this book easily lend themselves to gold wire—but master the techniques in silver before attempting gold work. The cost demands it! For chain applications, 18-karat or 14-karat gold is best. Because silver is easier to manipulate than gold, use the next smaller gauge of gold wire than the silver recommended in the projects. Gold is sold by the pennyweight rather than by the ounce.

Copper is relatively inexpensive and almost as soft to work with as sterling silver, but it quickly becomes work hardened and brittle, and requires frequent annealing to keep it from breaking. Copper must be coated with wax or varnish to prevent tarnishing. Be sure to wash your hands after handling copper for long periods of time; it can be poisonous. There is no copper-colored solder, but silver solder works well.

Metals such as aluminum, niobium, nickel, and platinum aren't really suitable for handmade chain making. Aluminum is quite brittle and is only joinable with a tungsten arc welder; niobium is only used in jewelry in an unsoldered form. Nickel is a metal many people are allergic to; it's only really useful for creating templates or working out design ideas. Platinum requires its own set of tools, is much harder to form by hand, and is very expensive. Platinum wire isn't available in as many thicknesses as are sterling silver and gold.

Of course, wire isn't the only material you can use. Try sheet metal to make links for endless possibilities. Mix different metals in the design of your chain. If a link can be made, it can be joined and turned into a hand-made chain! Achieve unusual results with mixed media such as plastic, leather, wood, clay, or any workable material. Once you work your way through these projects, you'll have the confidence to design your own chains and link your life with art.

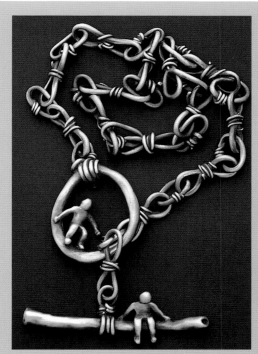

Hadar Jacobson, *Look Out!,* 2003. 22 in. (55.9 cm). Fine silver metal clay; hand fabricated, assembled, fired, oxidized. Photo by artist

Studio Essentials

To make the projects in this book you'll need a few tools and supplies and a basic knowledge of how to use them. Crafting handmade chains demands a few different tool setups, so I've found it very efficient to use work areas, or "stations," as I design, fabricate, and finish each piece. It's nice to have space dedicated to these activities, though you don't need much room. Chain making is a messy process, so consider using a home basement, garage, or laundry room rather than a corner of the living room. You'll need a sink nearby, for water and to keep the studio space clean, and three work surfaces. You could spring for fancy prefabricated jeweler's workbenches, but any tabletop will do. Flame-retardant flooring, such as concrete or tile, is essential. Adequate ventilation will pull any fumes out of your work environment. And you'll need good lighting at all stations; clip lamps provide portable and versatile task lighting.

Organizing and setting up all the materials, tools, and supplies at each station can be done in a variety of ways. For clutter-free work surfaces, pegboard and appropriate hooks make inexpensive tool holders. Old shoeboxes, glass jars, and toolboxes are great for storing loose or awkward items. Check with suppliers if you're stumped; they often have specialized storage solutions for jewelers' needs.

The chemicals, sharp tools, and flammable gases in the studio make it necessary to safeguard the workspace from children and pets. Read and keep on hand the Material Safety Data Sheets that come with any chemicals you use; these describe the ingredients; rate their toxicity, if any; and tell you how to safely handle and dispose of the material. The suppliers are required to provide this information, but you can also request it from the manufacturer via the Internet or by phone.

All metal-working tools should be handled with acute awareness. Tie back long hair, don't wear loose clothing around motors or flames, and keep track of your fingers. Use grounded extension cords or outlet bars and don't attempt to rewire or electrically alter any machinery. A fully stocked first aid kit in the studio is a must. And, because of the potential dangers, if you're working alone, have someone check on you every few hours. If you want to be sure of having years of fun in your studio, consider safety first.

Joanna Gollberg, *Nil Earrings and Necklace,* 2004. Necklace, 18 in. (45.7 cm); earrings, 2 in. (5.1 cm). Sterling silver; fabricated. Photo by Stewart O'Shields

The Creation Station

This area is the main hub of your creative work, where you'll use various hand tools to shape and work raw materials into links. Keep it clean, and have a sketchbook nearby to capture your inspirations.

Measuring Tools

Visually, the difference between the wire gauges is subtle. A Brown & Sharpe (or American) wire gauge will ensure you're using wire of the right diameter for the project (for British equivalents, see the Key to Wire Gauges on page 106). To make accurate cuts and visual notations on silver, use a fine-point permanent marker; the ink rubs off easily, or burns off during soldering. Use a 6-inch (15.2 cm) ruler (with markings up to 1/16-inch [1.6 mm] increments) to measure lengths of wire. A larger measuring tool always comes in handy for sizing final lengths of chain. To keep jewelry links organized and clean, put them in small zipping plastic bags.

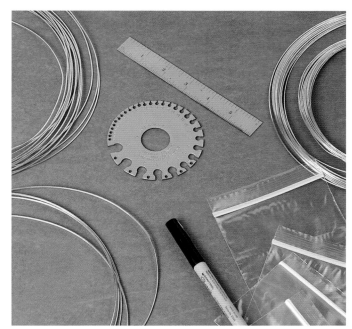

Basic tools at the creation station are a wire gauge, a ruler, silver coils, zipping plastic bags, and a permanent marker.

Pliers and Cutters

Pliers are used to hold onto wire and also act as a mandrel (see Shaping and Filing Tools on page 12) for shaping it. They give you enough torque, or twisting force, to bend the wire with relatively little effort. Pliers are sold with different kinds of hinging mechanisms. Box joint, or parallel, pliers are particularly helpful for the beginner chain maker because they grab the wire squarely and ensure more control over the shaping process. Lap joint pliers have a tapered jaw angle and are less expensive, but they take more practice to keep the link from warping.

Each of the jeweler's pliers you'll be using has a specially shaped tip, or nose

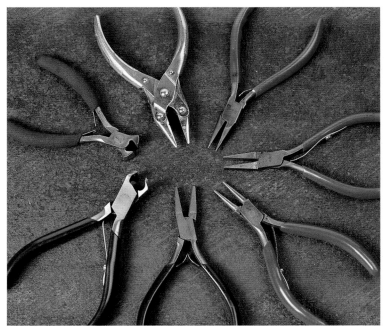

The basic hand tools (from clockwise top): box joint chain nose, lap joint chain nose, flat nose, round nose, half-round nose, large end cutters, and small end cutters

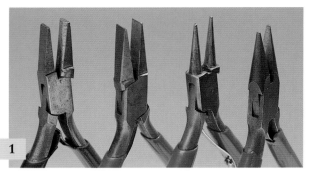

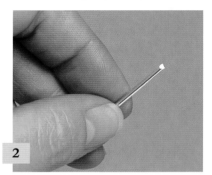

1

The greatest control over the shaping process is achieved with a variety of pliers' tips; shown here (from left to right) are half round, flat, round, and chain box-joint types.

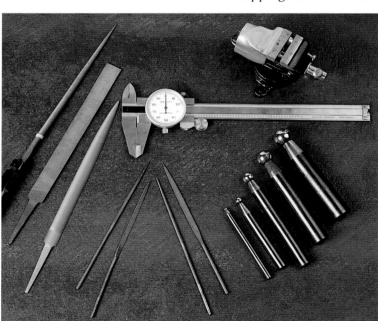

2

The large burr made with regular cutters creates extra filing work.

(see photo 1). Shaping wire is easier if you use the pliers most appropriate for the design. Round nose pliers are used to make tiny curves and small rounded shapes. For softer curves and larger round shapes, use half round–nose pliers; they're also great for straightening bent wires. Flat nose pliers shape larger flat lines or squared angles, and chain nose pliers do the same on a smaller scale (they're also great for holding small parts and for joining links). Whatever the style, make sure the pliers' jaws aren't serrated because they'll mar the links and make more polishing work for you.

Check the maximum gauge that your wire cutters are rated to cut. For this book, 14 gauge is the heaviest wire you'll use. Either end cutters or side cutters are best for cutting into tighter spots; choose one with a flush or semi-flush cut. Flush cutters are designed to leave the ends of the wire with a relatively small burr. You won't have to spend as much time filing rough ends as you would with the large burr from a regular cutter (see photo 2). When you do have to file, a set of needle files and hand files, in round, flat, half round, square, triangular, and oval shapes, will come in handy.

Shaping and Filing Tools

Wrapping silver wire around a round *mandrel* makes circles, the basic shape for many of the projects. To create all the chains, you'll need five mandrels in the following sizes: 1/4 inch (6 mm), 3/8 inch (9.5 mm), 1/2 inch (1.3 cm), 5/8 inch (1.6 cm), and 3/4 inch (1.9 cm), and in order to handle them comfortably, buy ones that are 4 to 5 inches (10.2 to 12.7 cm) long. A round needle file handle can be used as a mandrel for the smallest links, or you could try a nail or other thick wire for the job. Any cylinder of the right size, if it's made of a hard enough material, can be used as a mandrel. To start out, use calipers to help you measure diameters; then you can piece together your own set of mandrels from found articles. Extra torque is sometimes needed for bending wire, so a vise can be helpful.

Tools used at the creation station (clockwise from top right): vise, caliper, mandrels, needle files, and hand files

Hammers and Blocks

Forging hammers and steel blocks are used to help create the final shape and texture of the metal. There are many types of forging hammers, each with its own uniquely shaped, polished-steel head. Choose a forging hammer with a small flat face in whatever weight feels best in your hand. I recommend hammers that weigh 4 to 6 ounces (112 to 168 g). If you are unsure which weight you'd prefer and need to order a hammer sight unseen, do your research at a local hardware store. Certain projects specify which type of forging hammer is best; otherwise, use any style flat-faced steel head you like.

A planishing hammer has a polished surface used for removing other hammer marks; in chain making applications this tool does the job of shaping the metal without creating extra polishing work. The riveting hammer is used for textured forging, but the round end of a ball peen hammer can also be used for such tasks. Use a flat rawhide or nylon hammer (not considered a forging tool) to shape links without marring them.

You'll also need a flat *bench block* made of tool steel. Put it on any sturdy tabletop with a thin rubber mat to keep it in place. For beginners, a flat block is preferable to a domed one because you're less likely to hammer a finger accidentally. If you have forging experience then, by all means, use what you're accustomed to. Always wear earplugs when hammering. You'll be amazed how much noise banging two steel tools together can make. (So will the family!) Wear eye protection, too; banging steel tools can create flying bits of metal.

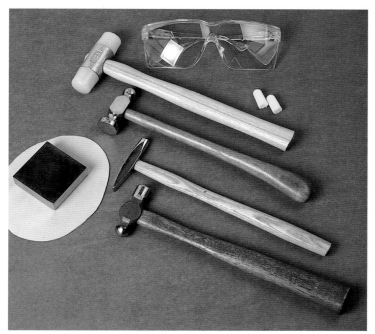

Forging tools and accessories (clockwise from top): safety glasses, earplugs, nylon hammer, planishing hammer, riveting hammer, ball peen hammer, and a bench block set on a thin rubber mat

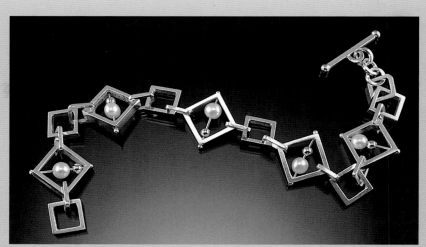

Danielle Miller-Gilliam, *Abacus Bracelet #10,* 2003. 7¹/₂ in. (19 cm). Sterling silver, 14-karat gold beads, pearls; hand fabricated, cast. Photo by artist

13

The Soldering Station

The soldering station is where you use fire to join two pieces of metal permanently. Keep the space free of flammables, such as paper, cloth, and the like.

The temperature of a jeweler's torch can exceed 1700°F (928°C), so the work surface here should be able to take the heat. Tile made of stone or ceramic material, or stainless steel, are great choices. On top of that surface, use one of the many kinds of heat blocks (ceramic and silica are common) or use ceramic firebrick to protect further the worktop from burning. I don't recommend charcoal for general soldering because this soft material will burn away with repeated use, leaving an ashy, uneven work surface. Charcoal's great, however, for melting silver. As long as it's flat and relatively hard, it can be used for chain making. You'll want a block that is, at the very least, 6 inches (15.2 cm) square.

Tools for soldering include (clockwise from top) a bowl with a lid for pickle, dry pickle, a clean-water rinse bowl, copper tongs, clean towels, a fuel tank and regulator, a large stone tile, a spark lighter, soldering pad, soldering block, third hand (with black base), tweezers (two styles shown), charcoal block, wire solder, torch in a stand, shaded goggles, and liquid flux in a spray bottle.

Safety is very important here because of the presence of torches, pressurized gasses, and the toxic fumes that are a by-product of the process. Keep a fire extinguisher handy and keep your wits about you. Also, this station gets dirty and should be under direct ventilation. Ventilation can be as simple as a blower that moves air away from you or as sophisticated as a professionally installed hood system. Talk to your local heating and air specialist if you need more information.

Soldering Tools and Supplies

Silver solders have different names to describe their melting temperatures and come in several forms (paste, sheet, and wire of different gauges). *Easy* solder melts at a lower temperature than does *medium* solder, but the color of medium is a better color match to sterling silver, so the solder joints are less visible. If you're a beginner, use 20-gauge easy wire solder until you're comfortable enough with soldering to try medium solder. *Flux*, a chemical compound, is always used first, to clean and protect silver so that solder

Essentials at the polishing station (clockwise from top): mesh basket, rotary tumbler with barrel, stainless steel shot, and ceramic media in a barrel, with its lid and gasket nearby

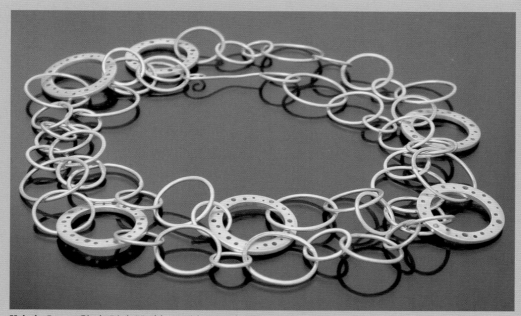

Kristin Lora, *Circle Link Necklace with Dotted Discs,* 2004. 32 in. (81.3 cm). Fine silver, sterling silver; hand fabricated, hand formed, hammered. Photo by artist

flows and adheres properly to it. In liquid form, flux can be sprayed or spritzed on, protecting every part of the chain (especially the joint) from the oxidization that occurs during soldering, and it saves time spent polishing.

Soldering chain elements requires that you use one or more special kinds of tweezers during the process. Soldering tweezers are either the familiar straight style or the squeeze-to-open cross-locking type, which these used to hold wire solder or links under a flame. They get warm, so look for heat-resistant grips. Small straight tweezers are used for positioning links on the soldering block before or after soldering them. A *third hand* is a type of stand that holds cross-locking tweezers, which hold elements in position while soldering.

Pickle solution cleans up *fire scale*, a black by-product of oxygen's interaction with copper at high heat. Choose the least toxic pickle that's available from your supplier; I recommend sodium bisulfate in granular form. The dry pickle, an acidic product, is added to water (never the other way around!) to make the solution. Although manufacturers recommend that pickle stay warm in a heated pot, you can reduce toxic fumes in the studio by keeping it in a glass bowl with a lid at room temperature. Use copper tongs to add or retrieve all items from the pickle. Steel or iron creates a reaction with pickle solution that causes items to copper plate, so don't ever let your stainless steel tweezers touch the solution. Rinse pickled jewelry in a bowl of plain cold water.

Sadie Wang, *Hammer Lines Textured Multi-Rectangle Necklace and Bracelet,* 2001. Necklace, 17 in. (43.2 cm); bracelet, 6¾ in. (17.1 cm). Sterling silver. Photo by John Lucas

Soldering Equipment

The soldering system is the main tool at the soldering station. It has relatively few parts, that should be assembled in the order in which they're discussed here. Two tanks hold compressed oxygen and dissolved acetylene; these make a nice hot flame when they're mixed together. Acetylene is the fuel gas; oxygen, the accelerant, makes the fuel burn hotter. This is often referred to as oxy/acetylene soldering. Store these pressurized tanks in restraints (you can chain them to a nearby wall) and keep them upright at all times. A two-stage regulator, one for each gas, controls the flow of gas from the tank and reduces it to a safe working level. The dial closer to the tank shows how much gas is in it, and the other dial indicates how much gas is coming out of the hose. The hose pressure is controlled with a small screw valve on the regulator. Hoses for both tanks should be long enough to provide maneuverability when soldering, and must be checked regularly for cracks and holes. Once a hose is used for a specific gas it must not be used for any other application.

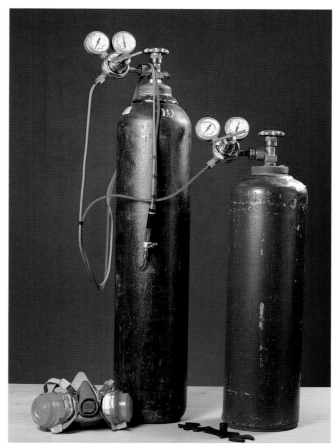

The oxy/acetylene system is comprised of two tanks, each with regulators: oxygen and acetylene, connected to the torch with the proper connecting hoses; a tank wrench and a respirator are also necessary.

A small torch, attached to the tanks by two hoses, has needle valves in its handle that allow you to further control the gas output. The two gases are mixed in the torch tip to form a flame when lit. The tip numbering system is simple; a larger tip number corresponds to a bigger flame. For these projects, use tip number 3 or 4. Soldering systems are designed in several sizes, depending on the size of the tank, so make sure that every component fits properly. Check with your supplier; often you can get a complete system for a better price than buying the parts individually. Read all the accompanying information on setup and use.

Soldering Safety

A few accessories are necessary for safe and comfortable soldering. Use a sparking flint lighter—never matches or a cigarette lighter—to light the fuel gas (i.e., the acetylene). The only flame here should be coming from the end of the torch. Shaded welding goggles or safety glasses, outfitted with a number 3 or 4 filter, will protect your eyes from the ultraviolet and infrared light waves that are emitted from flames. They usually fit over eyeglasses, if you wear them. Please protect your eyes—you only get one pair.

Extra-bright task lighting will help you see better while you work with shaded goggles on. A torch hanger can hold a lit torch should you need to put it down momentarily during soldering. Be aware that burning gasses, flux, solder, silver, and pickle solution fumes are all dangerous to breathe. Ventilation is only one part of the solution to reduce exposure to toxic chemicals and fumes. You'll also need to wear a respirator that filters out particles, vapors, and chemical fumes. A common dust, or "comfort," mask won't protect you from harmful exposure.

Pressurized gases are flammable, combustible, and potentially dangerous if handled incorrectly. Keep your flame away from the system. Hand-tighten the tank fittings with a tank wrench, and never oil the fittings. If you're a beginner and have never soldered before, visit a local library, studio jeweler, or welding shop to learn more about the oxy/acetylene soldering system and how it works. The supplier should also be able to answer your questions. If you presently have a propane or air/acetylene soldering system, you can use it, but you may have trouble with some of the soldering projects because those soldering systems tend to make a large flame instead of a pinpoint one, which allows greater control over the soldering process.

Sadie Wang, Double Circle Series, 2001. 17 in. (43.2 cm). Sterling silver. Photo by R.H. Hensleigh

The Polishing Station

This station is another messy one, so keeping it near the soldering station makes sense. A nearby sink comes in handy, too, but you can use buckets of clean water instead.

Flexible Shaft Tool

The flexible shaft tool is similar in function to the kind of household drill that has interchangeable buffers and drill bits. The flexible shaft is different because its handpiece provides fine control over your work. A foot pedal speed controller keeps both hands free, much like a sewing machine's pedal. The main part of the system is a relatively small, heavy motor, to which is attached a long, flexible shaft that ends with a hand piece. A chuck key opens the jaw to insert various tools, each of which must be mounted on its own special type of mandrel. The hand piece simply snaps into the end of the shaft and can be easily removed or changed. Powerful motors and a lot of accessories are available, but a basic model is fine for chain making. Stay alert when using this machine because hair and clothing can get twisted around the fast-rotating tools.

The machine should be placed at a height you can comfortably work with because you should avoid bending, and possibly kinking, the flexible shaft. Also available are specially designed flexible shaft hangers that allow the system to be easily repositioned. A wooden bench pin attaches to the front of the workbench so you can rest the work against it, allowing you to gain full access to all sides. The pin is a good place to do drilling, if need be, because it's more easily replaced than the tabletop.

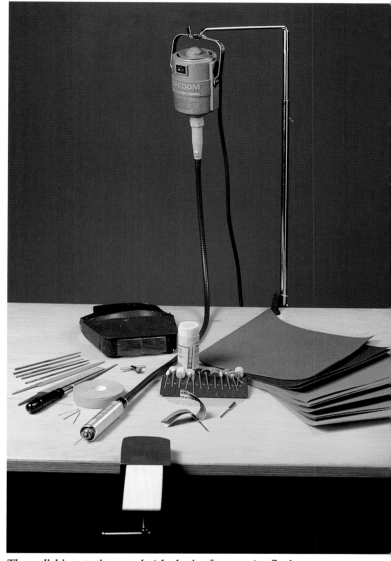

The polishing station needs (clockwise from top) a flexible shaft motor (hanging from a shaft hanger); sandpapers; a sandpaper mandrel (two are shown); a wooden bench pin (affixed in a vice to the edge of the table); a flexible shaft hand piece; self-adhesive bandage tape; various drill bits, hand files, and needle files; a magnifying visor; the hand piece's chuck key; metal lubricant; and a set of polishing wheels.

Accessories

Very small metal twist drill bits should drill a slightly larger hole than the wire that will be passing through it. Use the chart below to match the drill bit diameter to your wire gauge.

Sterling Silver Gauge/Drill Bit Equivalents

20 gauge	18 gauge	16 gauge	14 gauge
.84 mm	1.04 mm	1.32 mm	1.7 mm

Metal lubricant is great for filing and drilling; it keeps friction at a minimum and increases the life of the cutting edge of the tool. Never use dull cutting tools because they can contribute to accidents and make the work harder than it should be.

You'll use sandpaper, from coarse (80 grit) to super-extra fine (8000 grit), and a sandpaper mandrel for several different tasks. You might find it more convenient to buy a set of papers that includes a selection of each grit. Use the coarser sandpapers (from 80 to 1000 grit) to shape and polish your steel hammers and bench blocks, and the finer grits (from 200 to 8000) on silver. Keep the papers you use to polish steel separate from the ones you use to polish silver. Steel particles can get pushed into silver, wreaking havoc on the finish.

The shape of a polishing wheel should match the shape of the crevice where the scratch is; often, flat wheels can be shaped to fit as needed. Check with the supplier for the availability of shapes and grits of polishing wheels, and keep a selection of coarse, medium, fine, and superfine wheels. Sandpaper and polishing wheels are usually made up of silicon and other materials that are harmful when inhaled. Even if you have a vacuum system or dust collector for heavier flying particles, you should still wear a respirator and protective eyewear. A thin layer of adhesive bandage tape is great for wrapping around your fingertips to provide extra grip on small items and to protect them from the heat that can develop when polishing or drilling metal.

A magnifying visor while you're polishing helps you get a closer view, to make sure that soldering joints are properly soldered and all scratches are polished out. Visors are available at different magnifying strengths, depending on your eyesight and the desired level of magnification.

Holly Masterson, *Links Alot,* 2004. Necklace, 16 in. (40.6 cm); bracelet, 7¹/₂ in. (19 cm). Sterling silver; hand fabricated. Photo by artist

Hand Files

For more control over how much metal you remove, hand files work better than the flex shaft. A set of hand files with medium to fine cutting teeth, in round, flat, and half-round shapes, is good for the overall shaping of larger links, while needle files in various shapes help remove metal from tight spots and crevices. Check with the supplier for the number of teeth per inch, because files are rated differently, depending on where they are made. Generally, the larger the rating number, the finer the cut.

Tumblers

A vibrating or rotary tumbler, consisting of a barrel filled with soapy water and media, or *shot*, plus your jewelry piece, must run for many hours, so buy a good quality machine. A vibratory tumbler shakes the barrel while a rotary tumbler rotates it; either is fine. Use a basic dishwashing detergent and water as an all-purpose lubricant for media and shot. Don't use scented or antibacterial soaps; their chemicals can alter results.

Hadar Jacobson, *Textures,* 2003. 22 in. (55.9 cm). Fine silver metal clay; hand fabricated, linked, fired, oxidized. Photo by artist

As the tumbler rotates, the tumbling media gently abrade the jewelry piece to its final finish. Depending on the finish you want, media are available in many different abrasions, and they may be made of ceramic, plastic, or stainless steel. The various shapes of the media ensure that every little nook and cranny of the design gets polished; use a medium to fine grit of ceramic or plastic media for satin or matte finishes. Stainless steel shot is used to attain a high polish. I don't recommend the carbon steel shot, because it requires special solutions and methods to keep the shot from rusting. Store stainless shot in plain water; it won't rust.

When the tumbling is done, rinse the shot of any dirt or abrasive particles. Make sure the mesh basket's weave is tight enough to keep the smallest pieces of shot from falling through the holes and clogging the sink's drain. When your silver chain comes out of the mesh basket, use soft towels to dry it. Be sure to keep these towels extra clean. Put the finished chain in a zipping plastic bag to keep it from tarnishing; you don't want anything to harm the final polish you worked so hard to get.

The next section covers the techniques necessary for successful tool, equipment, and material handling. If you're a beginner, the how-to information and photographs will demonstrate the methods you need to make the projects. For more experienced readers, a review of basic techniques will refresh your memory and give you insight into the methods that are specific to chain making.

Sterling silver wire is easy to work with once you have a little experience and understand some basic principles of the way it reacts to what you do to it. It's a surprisingly plastic material, with both rigidity and flexibility.

In this section, I'll demonstrate the basic techniques of bending, soldering, and polishing wire as they relate to chain making. Use it as a handy reference if you encounter any difficulties; most of them are simply solved. Getting a feel for working with wire only comes with practice. So dive in!

Working with Wire

The nature of wire is rather odd: It's a linear form but has three-dimensional qualities, too. Yet from this very ordinary material you can, once you understand its unique characteristics, make marvelous, fanciful, soaring jewelry pieces. The challenge is to wrestle the straight line of the plain wire into a series of linked shapes that together create the harmonious form of a finished chain.

Cutting Wire

To cut short lengths of wire, slide the wire alongside a ruler and mark the length to be cut with your permanent marker. For projects with lots of pieces to be measured, mark all the needed parts and then cut them apart with wire cutters. When using wire cutters, position the wire in the jaws of the cutter squarely (that is, at a 90-degree angle to the wire); and be sure to hold onto both sides of it. If you could watch your cutters in action with a microscope, you'd see that only part of the wire is cut by the blade and the rest *shears*, or breaks, off. The energy from the break causes the wire to shoot out from the cutters in both directions.

Filing

Use a flat file and imagine you're filing your fingernails. It's that simple. Use light pressure and draw the file back and forth along its length, squarely to the end of the wire, as shown in photo 3. Using too much pressure, or short strokes, can result in bent and misshapen wire. An angled stroke will make it nearly impossible to solder the ends into a strong joint. Feel the end of the wire with your fingertip to make sure it has been filed smoothly.

Shaping Warm-Up

Cut a 2-inch (5 cm) length of straight wire and bend it randomly with any pliers, then straighten the wire, matching the shape of the pliers to the shape of the bend. Use flat or chain nose pliers for angular bends and round or half round pliers for curves. Grasp the wire at the bend with the pliers and use your hand to apply pressure in the direction opposite the bend. Focus on one bend from one angle at a time, straightening it completely before moving on to another.

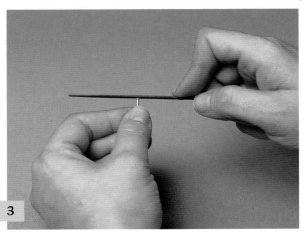

3

Keep the file flat and square to the end of the wire.

Shaping

Wire from a supplier will most likely arrive on a spool or in a large coil. If you need to straighten out such a slight curve, use your fingers to pull along its length as you apply gentle, even pressure against the curve, in the same way you might use scissors to curl a ribbon. Anchor one end with flat nose pliers while you pull it straight (see photo 4). The multiple bends—all at slightly different angles—that you'll use to create a link can make correcting a problem quite a challenge. Beginning wire shapers often inadvertently make warped links. Even if you're not new at this, the best way to work is to watch the wire-shaping progression from two different planes or views as you shape it.

Whenever a wire is bent or shaped, interesting changes take place inside the metal. A perfect illustration of these inner molecular movements is in the bent neck of a flexible straw (see photo 5). The molecules at the outer part of the curve are stretched and on the inside they're compressed. When you bend (or, more accurately, compress) and stretch the wire, it becomes *work hardened*. Occasionally, the wire may become so brittle and misshapen that you'd be better off starting with fresh wire rather than trying to salvage it by annealing.

Josephine Jacobsmeyer, *5 Link Bracelets,* 2004.
Each, 7¼ in. (18.4 cm). Sterling silver, cabochons; hand fabricated, chased.
Photo by Don Casper, Casper Photoworks

Bending Warm-Up

Cut a 2-inch (5 cm) length of straight wire and, using round nose pliers, bend it in half, so that the ends of the wires meet each other exactly. Adjust any unevenness by unbending the leg that's too short, then rebending the leg that was too long.

4

Straightening a wire by pulling *against* the curved tension

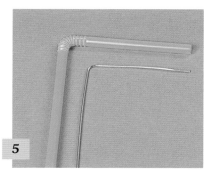

5

The stretched-and-crunched parts of a bend in a drinking straw are similar to the kinds of molecular changes that occur in the bent area of a piece of wire.

23

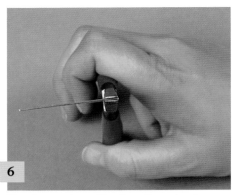

6

Shaping a wire with pliers (top view)

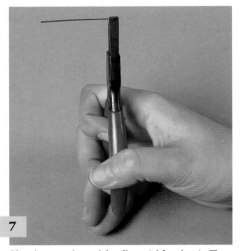

7

Shaping a wire with pliers (side view). To maintain control over the shaping process, keep the wire positioned at a 90-degree angle to the pliers' jaws.

Wire shaping requires that you learn how to use pliers and your hands together, at the same time. To avoid warping it, keep the wire positioned in the jaw of the pliers at a 90-degree angle, checking both the top and the side views (see photos 6 and 7). To make a bend, you need an *anchor* for the wire and a *shaper*. The pliers can act as the anchor while your hands shape the metal, or vice versa. Either way, use just enough pressure on the pliers to hold the wire while bending it; don't grip them too tightly.

Circles

To make circles, a length of wire is first wrapped around a mandrel to create a coil, using your hand to do the job. Place the mandrel in your left hand, lay the length of wire midway over the mandrel, and clamp it at the midpoint with your thumb (see photo 8). If you lack sufficient strength, clamp the mandrel into a vise. Use your other hand to grasp the wire close to the mandrel and wrap it snugly around the mandrel, sliding your grip down the wire as you go and pulling on the wire to create a little bit of tension (see photo 9). Be sure to align the wire with the last wrap and as close as possible to it without overlapping.

To finish making the circles, flip the mandrel around, twist the coil so it's tight against the mandrel again, and finish the wrapping with the other half of the wire. The final coil will look like a spring (see photo 10). If you find that you've made a coil of uneven circles, tighten the coil back onto the mandrel by twisting it against the mandrel in the direction of the wrap.

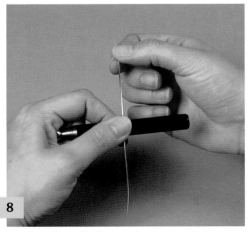

8

Starting the coil. Clamp the center of the wire to the mandrel with your thumb.

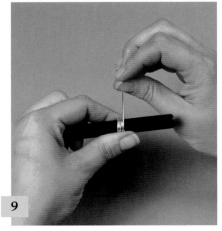

9

Keep tension in the wire as you wrap by gently pulling on it.

10

A finished coil of circles, still on the mandrel

As you near the end the wire, it becomes more difficult to wrap by hand. Round nose or half round–nose pliers can help with extra leverage to finish shaping the end of the wire (see photo 11). The coil unravels a bit when you let go because sterling silver is elastic. This coil expansion has been accounted for in the project measurements. When you create your own designs, use mandrels smaller than the desired circle diameter. Test wrap your mandrels to see what size circle is made.

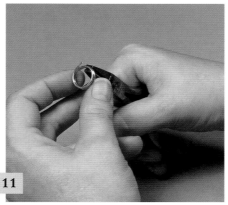

11

With round nosed pliers, shape the end of the wire to match the curve of the coil.

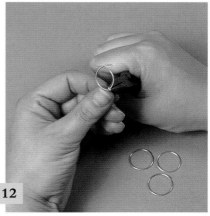

12

Bending an open circle at its midpoint

Finally, cut the coil into neat, ready-to-use circles. The skill levels necessary for the projects that use unaltered circles range from super-simple (see the Circle chain on page 55) to advanced (such as the Layered Circles chain on page 100). Some projects, such as the Spiral (page 70) and the Teardrop (page 72) chains, utilize a gentle curve in their designs, and so you'll start the shaping from an open circle rather than from straight wire. To preserve the circle's curve when working on one of these designs, apply pressure only to the point on the wire directly next to the pliers, and make the necessary bends only once (see photo 12). If drastic corrections have to be made, the overall curve of the link will be altered, too. It's a lot easier to make a bend in the right spot the first time than it is to correct it so that the error isn't noticeable.

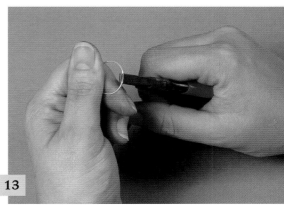

13

Keep the circle's round shape by holding it along the wire when bending.

Some circles are closed with solder before the shaping is done. Closed-circle shaping is like playing with a rubber band; when you pull on one part of the circle, it moves and affects the rest of the shape. Working with closed circles is useful for achieving shapes that would be harder to reproduce repetitively from straight wire. When you're shaping a closed circle, hold onto it along the wire rather than across it, so as not to change the shape of the circle (see photo 13). Apply direct pressure to the wire, against the pliers' jaws. A light squeeze with flat nose pliers can flatten out a section of a circle. You'll get plenty of practice with closed circles in chain projects such as the Amoeba (page 56) or the more challenging Geometric (page 58).

Loops

Loops are small circles shaped from straight wires. They're often placed at the end of a wire to provide simple joinery for the chain, such as in the Tadpole design on page 74, or employed as a decorative element, as seen in the Wiggle chain on page 63. Use round nose pliers to make all your loops. The pliers' jaws are conically shaped, with a small tip that graduates to a larger base. (Half round–nose pliers can be used to hand-shape larger loops if the base of your round nose pliers is too small.)

To create a *side loop*, grasp the end of the wire with the jaw of the pliers (see photo 14), positioning the wire at the point on the pliers that will give you the size loop you want. Place the thumb of your free hand along the wire, next to the jaws of the pliers, and push your thumb against the pliers as you turn the pliers against the wire. Reposition the pliers' grip on the wire until the end of the loop touches the rest of the wire (see photo 15).

For a *straight loop*, first make a side loop. Grasp the wire just inside the loop but beyond the point where it contacts the rest of the wire and bend it to a 90-degree angle (see photo 16). The U-shaped *half loop* is a partially completed side loop. Half loops can be left that way or bent at a 90-degree angle to create a *straight half loop* (see photo 17), which I used in the Demi-Circle project on page 77.

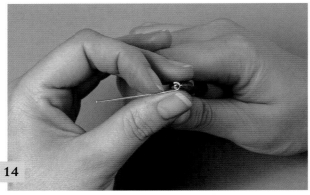

14

Starting a side loop with round nosed pliers, use your thumb to apply pressure against both the wire and pliers.

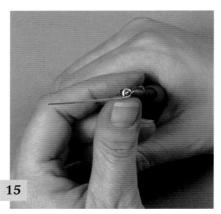

15

Closing the side loop

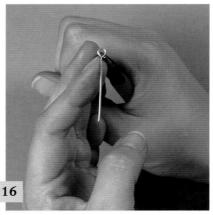

16

A small bend changes a side loop into a straight one.

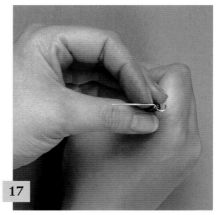

17

Bend a half loop into a straight half loop in similar fashion to the full loop.

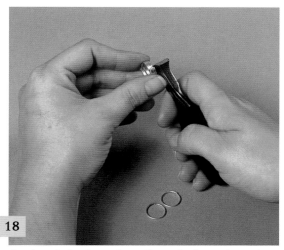

18

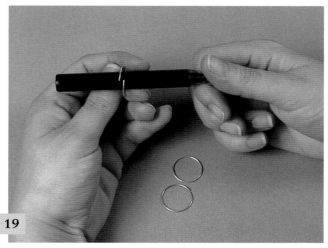

19

Cutting circles from the coil evenly, keep the end cutter positioned squarely to the wire.

Once the circle is cut from the coil, its ends are offset and must be aligned.

Cutting Circles

To cut circles from a coil, match one cut end to the next bit of coil (see photo 18). The circles will have offset ends (see photo 19), which can overlap and catch on each other during the shaping process, altering the shape of the circle. Because silver wire is so malleable, it's surprisingly easy to warp a circle out of shape inadvertently, and difficult to get it back into just the right shape and size. So, gently open the circle sideways, as described in the section on Alignment on page 28, to make sure the ends are clear of each other before shaping or filing.

Kathleen Lynagh House, *Q Necklace*, 2004. 16 in. (40.6 cm). Sterling silver; cast, polished. Photo by Hap Sakwa

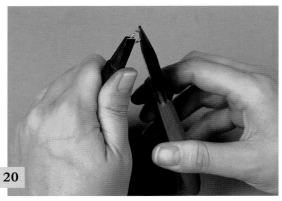

20

Use pliers to twist small circles open or closed.

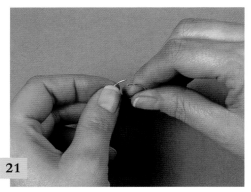

21

A larger circle is easily twisted open or closed by hand.

Alignment

All loops and circles have to be closed and aligned before they're soldered into a nice, solid solder joint. To keep the shape of the circle or loop, twist the ends of the wire sideways to open and close them. This helps circles and loops keep their round shape as you continue to work with them. Smaller loops and circles may need the extra torque that's achieved by using two pliers (see photo 20). Larger circles are easily aligned by hand (see photo 21). To align the joint correctly, you may need to swing the ends past each other, opposite the metal's tension, before the ends will rest naturally together. You should check the ends' alignment from top and side views. It's important when aligning the joint that the placement doesn't rely on forced tension. A forced joint will spring apart with the slightest bump. You may need a magnifying visor to make sure that it's correctly aligned and that the ends are touching.

Holly Masterson, *Circle of Squares,* 2004. Necklace, 15 in. (38.1 cm); bracelet, 7 in. (17.8 cm). Sterling silver; hand fabricated, hand-hammered finish. Photo by artist

Making All the Shapes Alike

Using *sense memory* and *visual cues* are two techniques for making duplicates of the same shape. Sense memory is a term that's mostly used by "Method" actors, who recall memories from their five senses to really feel and understand a character's emotions. In this instance, I mean that you should use your sense of touch, both muscular and tactile, to physically remember how hard you pushed on a wire or how much you twisted your pliers or hand. You'll find that because of sense memory, making the last few links will be easier than the first ones.

Visual cues come from the positions and placements of your hands, wire, and tools. You should hold your hands and wire in the same relative position as you shape each link. Noting visual details—such as just where along the wire you make the first, second, or third bend and just where on the jaw of the pliers you grasp the wire— helps you shape your links so they are all the same. You can use a permanent marker to mark those key spots along the pliers and wires. Marks on tools wear off with use, so keep an eye on the mark before it's gone. If you can draw the link or shape to scale, you can lay your wire over the drawing and follow the lines, slowly shaping it as you go.

Cold Forging

Cold forging means hammering metal at room temperature, and silver is soft enough to do so. *Forging* makes wire stronger by work hardening it, creates variations in line thickness, and adds sparkle and visual interest to the material. Hammers and bench blocks are the tools used to help further enhance the shape and texture of the metal. A planishing hammer, for example, is used to forge wires smoothly. Whatever nicks, scratches, or marks are on the surface of the hammer and bench block will be transferred to the metal—for better or worse. For a smooth finish, be sure to keep both hammer and block well polished, filing away any sharp edges they might have.

22

A small abrasive wheel was used to cut the texture on the hammer head.

Spot forging is a technique that's used in most of the projects to flatten and widen round wire. Of course there's always the option not to hammer the links or to alter the forging instructions to suit your design.

Any hammer or block can be textured, then used to stamp texture onto metal (see photo 22). The small, rectangular face of a riveting

Hammering Warm-Up

Cut a 2-inch (5 cm) length of any gauge straight wire and hammer it, keeping the wire as straight as possible. If you inadvertently create a curve or a bend in the wire, remember that the innermost area of the bend is compressed and the outermost side is stretched. To correct the problem with the hammer, which can only stretch metal, aim for the inner (compressed) area of the curve to straighten it.

hammer, held at a 45-degree angle to the block, is used for texturing links in the Oval Stack chain on page 82 and the Joined Snakes chain on page 85.

A rawhide or nylon hammer will help flatten any warped or misshapen links without adding any texture or changing the thickness of the wire. It's important that you learn to use pliers to correct problems, so use this method only as a last resort, if pliers can't fix the shape.

Hammer Control

In jewelry making, you should wield your hammer in a very intentional yet relaxed way. Hold the hammer comfortably in your hand at the end of the handle; don't let your grip creep up the handle. Hold the hammer loosely and let the weight of the hammer fall, guided by your arm. Your arm will quickly tire if you grip it tightly in an effort to force heavy blows. And it will take some practice to gain control over where the hammer's head lands.

Hold your links flat on the steel block with light fingertip pressure, but keep your fingers off the block itself (see photo 23). Use a straight, up-and-down hammer blow, keeping the head of the hammer parallel to the surface of the block, as shown in photo 24. Held at an angle, the hammer will strike the steel block before the link. Let the link and the hammer interact without too much pressure from you, or you'll feel every blow of the hammer in your fingertips or cause the link to become misshapen. Finally, don't try to flatten balled wire (described in the next section) too quickly; hard, fast hammer blows can cause cracks in them.

23

Grasp the link firmly but keep your fingers off the block.

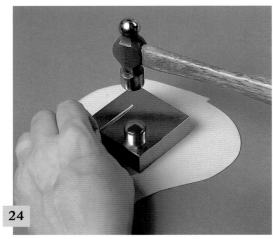

24

Be mindful of the angle of the hammer's head to the block.

Playing with Fire

When you're ready to solder, open the acetylene tank valve a quarter- or half-turn and open the oxygen tank valve all the way. Adjust each regulator's adjusting screw to 3 PSI (.207 bar) for acetylene and 8 PSI (.552 bar) for oxygen. Now you're ready to light the torch. There are two needle valves on the torch. Open the acetylene valve first and light it with a spark lighter, then slowly add oxygen to the flame. Notice that adding oxygen causes the flame to lose its bushy orange color. When two cones of light appear—a smaller cone of white light and a larger blue one, as shown in photo 25— you've created the ideal mixture of oxygen and acetylene. If you continue to add oxygen, you'll notice the flame seems to be forced out of the torch's tip, with the two different colored cones merging into one very small and bright one (see photo 26). This kind of flame is too hot and will dirty your metal unnecessarily.

During the soldering, the blue cone portion of the flame should hover over the metal without touching it. The greatest heat is just beyond, not in, the tip of the cone. Because the gas pressure may change unexpectedly, monitor the flame throughout the process. To extinguish the torch, first close the torch oxygen valve before closing the acetylene valve. When you're done for the day, extinguish the flame at the torch and then turn off the main tank valves. Reopen the torch valves to release any gasses in the hoses (away from you), and then close them for the final time.

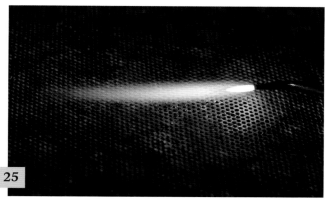

The right mix of oxygen and acetylene produces a "good" flame.

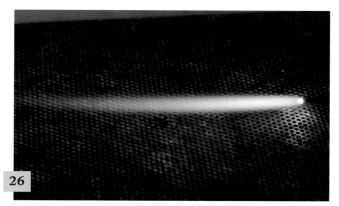

Too much oxygen creates a "bad" flame; note its sharply defined white cone.

Soldering Setup

To solder many pieces efficiently, it's useful to set up the links on the soldering block. You'll be instructed to "rotate the joints" so that they're clear of any neighboring links, easily visible, and accessible. To do this, hold the chain at one end and let it dangle. With your other hand, grasp the chain just below your hand and rotate the first joint into view with your thumb. Keep light tension in the chain and move your hand down the length of it, stopping to rotate each joint into view. Once aligned, maintain the light tension as you lay the chain on the soldering block. Lay rows of individual links on the block so they face in the same direction and give each row a little clearance. As you solder, use tweezers to shift solder joints, which may be hot, into view.

Successful Soldering

For beginners, soldering is often the most intimidating part of the process. Get comfortable with the equipment by test melting and soldering pieces of scrap first. Make a few extra links just in case you accidentally melt your wire work. A few guidelines can help put you in control by giving you an understanding of how actions cause reactions.

Flux is sprayed on before silver is soldered. It helps clean and protect the metal, and makes the solder flow and adhere better, so use it on every piece. Always.

The intensity of the flame is an important factor in the soldering process. Generally, the flame should get the metal to the soldering point within a window of 4 to 6 seconds. If it's ready faster than that, the joint will melt before you can solder it, and if it takes longer than 6 seconds the metal will get dirty and the solder won't flow properly. Solder melts on contact with hot silver, so heat the silver, not the solder. If solder melts before the joint is ready, too much solder will be laid at the joint. Only bring the solder into the flame once the metal is hot enough. How will you know? Look at the flux as you heat the piece. As the flux warms, it turns opaque white, but clears as it gets hotter. Simultaneously, the silver appears shiny and this is the exact moment to solder, before the metal melts.

To change the flame's size, use a different tip or adjust the torch

Ellen Vontillius, Untitled, 2002. 16 in. (40.6 cm).
Sterling silver, freshwater pearls; hand fabricated, cast.
Photo by Randall Smith

valves or the regulator screw valves. Remember that heavier gauge wire needs a hotter flame; be sure to test the flame every time before you solder a different gauge wire. With practice you'll get a feel for how big the flame size needs to be in relation to the heat and window of time that are necessary.

It's important to know that solder flows only to the hottest part of the piece. If solder flows away from a joint, the heat was misdirected. The shape and thickness of the wire work makes a difference in the way wire heats up and how the flame should be directed. And because a flame's heat path extends outward in a straight line, it can be easy to melt the wire before the joint itself is hot enough. Incorrect joint alignment can also cause unintentional melting or ugly solder joints. Occasionally you'll be instructed to use a horizontal or vertical flame to reduce the risk of melted links.

As you solder two ends of a wire, such as a circle, both ends of the wire must be heated at the same time. A very slight sweeping motion of the flame over the joint ensures even heating. To solder the end of a wire to the middle of a wire, as for a side loop, point the flame and its path at the point in the middle of the wire that's just beyond the intersection of the joint (see photo 27). Unless the heat path is altered, the end of a wire always gets hotter before the middle does.

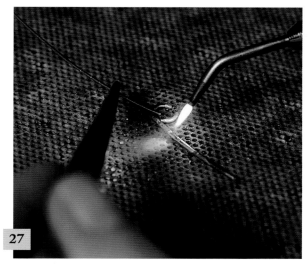

27

Successful soldering requires proper flame direction.

A proper flame comes straight out of the torch tip. Tips are easily damaged if dropped and can also get clogged with bits of dirt. If you notice a fishtail or crooked flame, the opening is obstructed or misshapen. Turn off the torch and inspect the tip. If the tip is damaged, lightly file it flat. If it's clogged, slide a thin round wire into the tip to loosen any debris.

Stick Soldering

A traditional solder pick and snippets of sheet solder can be used for all of the projects in this book, but they aren't ideal for chain making. To speed up time spent soldering the many joints in a chain, it's very useful to learn how to stick solder. Stick solder looks like wire and you hold it with cross-locking tweezers, lightly brushing or sweeping it across the joint. Done at just the right moment, this technique pulls just the right amount of solder from the stick, making a quick, perfect solder joint. The key here is to *brush* the end of the wire against the hot joint. If you let the solder linger at the joint, you'll leave a bump of excess solder. If the metal isn't hot enough, the sweeping action might shift the joint. Finally, if stick solder freezes to the joint, the joint was not quite hot enough; the stick wicked some of the heat, melted slightly, and then hardened.

To ensure that solder flowed over the entire joint, inspect all sides of the solder joints before placing the piece in the pickle. (Sometimes you may need to reheat the solder to the flow point.) Place a hot item in the pickle solution only after it loses its red glow; hot metal can spit and splash the acid onto you. Also, I recommend using room-temperature pickle, although it takes longer to remove the black or coppery residue from silver's surface than does heated pickle. Often, you can let the pickle do its work while you go on to another part of the process.

28

Watch the joint for the moment that the solder flows.

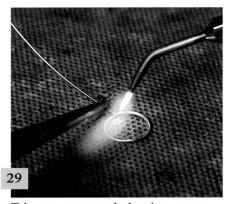

29

Take care not to melt the piece as you unstick the solder.

Quick-Fix Tips

If you solder two links together by accident, pull away the flame and allow the piece to cool slightly. Flux the joint. Grasp one of the links in a third-hand tweezers; grasp the other link with your hand tweezers (see photo 28). Heat up the joint until the solder flows, and wiggle the link in your hand tweezers. At the point of solder flow, when the links have separated, remove the flame and allow the solder to harden as you wiggle the link. Check that the solder on each separated link is smooth.

If the stick of solder freezes at the joint, immediately pull away the flame and let it cool slightly. Grasp the stuck stick of solder as close to the joint as possible with tweezers (see photo 29). Reheat only the metal, concentrating the flame near, not at, the joint or the stick of solder. As the solder in the joint heats and melts, quickly snap the stick away. Allow the remaining solder at the joint to melt and flow smooth.

Excess solder in a solder joint is easily fixed. Cut and flux a few ³⁄₄-inch (1.9 cm) pieces of 20- and 18-gauge sterling silver wire. Heat up the problem joint to the flow point and drag a heated silver wire piece across the joint. The extra solder will flow off the joint and onto the wire piece. Repeat with fresh wire as needed. Be sure to put used pieces with your scrap metal so you don't mistakenly reuse it, which would add more solder to a joint.

Balling Wire

Balling the end of a piece of wire is really simple and kind of fun. Heat the end of the wire until the capillary action of the molten metal causes it to roll itself into a ball. You won't need to file the end before you do so.

Actually, you can make two kinds of balls with wire. If a wire is melted while lying on a flat soldering block, you'll have a flat ball (see photo 30). To make a fully round ball, use cross-locking tweezers in a third hand to hold the wire vertically in the air. Heat the bottom end of the wire until it melts. The size of the ball depends on how long the heat is allowed to melt the wire, but it should never be more than three times the wire's original thickness. If you melt the top of the wire, gravity will pull the ball to one side. The projects that use balls are the Wiggle, Bar, Spiral, and Butterfly chains (see pages 63, 66, 70, and 100, respectively).

Connector pins are made from short pieces of wire balled on both ends. One end of the pin is balled and inserted into a hole in a link that's just large enough to accommodate it, then the other end is balled. The Scallop chain on page 68 uses such a joining device. Pin joints, such as those used in the Paddle chain (page 91), are part of the overall shape of the link; one balled end joins it to the next link.

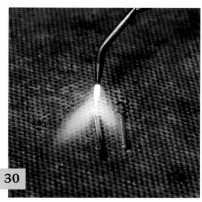

30

Be prepared to stop the melting just *before* the ball becomes the intended size.

Joanna Gollberg, *Resonance,* 2004. 7¹/₂ in. (19 cm). Sterling silver, freshwater pearls; fabricated. Photo by Stewart O'Shields

Making It Shine

Because silver is a soft metal, it can get scratched or marred when you're working with it. Work through the project steps and collect all the links to polish them at one time. *Area polish* the individual links before assembling the chain (see below). Once they're polished, continue to assemble the chain. If the chain is marred after assembly, polish the chain only by hand with sandpaper.

A motorized polishing tool can catch on the assembled chain, turning it into a safety hazard. If you need to use the flex shaft tool, disassemble the chain before you polish the marred links, then reassemble it. As a general rule, it's easier to prevent scratching and marring than it is to remove them. If the completed chain is unmarred, it can go straight to the all-over polishing method (see page 37).

Area Polishing

There are numerous polishing products and compounds available that aid in polishing metals; it's mostly a question of preference. Sandpaper is the simplest and most economical. When polishing marks from metal, assess the scratch damage and use only the finest grit necessary to remove the mark. Follow with even finer grits until

Kristin Lora, *Full Circle Necklace*, 2003. 16 in. (40.6 cm).
Fine silver; hand fabricated, soldered, hammered.
Photo by artist

the scratches are gone. Unlike the grit used for a polishing wheel, sandpaper grit tends to wear away as it's being used, so you're not as likely to overdo it. Polishing wheels are useful for getting into small or awkward crevices. When polishing with either paper or wheels, always change the direction of the drag of the polishing material over the metal. If left in one spot, the polishing action will put grooves in the metal.

All-Over Polishing

A tumbler is the final, easy polishing tool because it works with gravity and time; the time you'll save will free you to make more jewelry. Tumblers can use different media for different purposes (see photo 31). When an all-over satin finish is desired, the abrasive surfaces of ceramic or plastic media are best. Stainless steel shot gives a highly polished finish and work hardens the chain like tiny polished hammers without altering the shape of the metal. Most of the projects have a polished finish that shows the hammer work to best effect. Satin finishes emphasize the overall shape of a piece. Feel free to finish the project chains any way you wish.

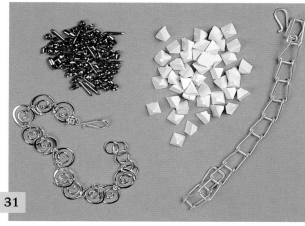

31

A high polish finish is created by stainless steel shot, and ceramic media produces a satin finish.

Drilling

Because the drill bits used in chain making are so thin and delicate, it's important to check that the bit is centered in the flexible shaft chuck before you drill. Once it's inserted and locked in, give it a little power and visually inspect the bit while looking straight at its tip. You'll notice the bit wobbles if it isn't properly centered.

It's important not to put too much pressure on the bit as you drill, or to change the drilling angle, which will cause the bit to snap and break. Hold the flexible shaft steadily on the surface and slowly increase the speed until the bit marks a spot and digs into the metal, then increase the drill speed and let the bit and gravity do the work (see photo 32). For a more secure start, use a center punch to lightly dimple the hole's location. Once the bit has passed through the metal, maintain the power as you back the bit out of the hole, keeping it at the same angle. If you pull out the bit at a different angle the round hole can become an oval, and the bit might break. The hole may have a sharp edge or burr around it, so be sure to lightly file or polish it off before assembling the links. The Bar, Scallop, and Paddle chains (see pages 66, 68, and 91) all require drilling.

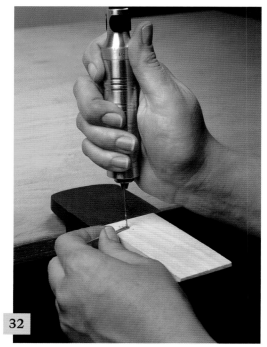

32

Hold the drill bit straight and square to the silver's surface.

Putting It All Together

A chain is generally made up of a few essential parts (see photo 33). Individual links are connected with each other, one way or another, to make up a chain. These links can be interconnected, linking one directly into the design of another, kind of like an M.C. Escher painting, or they can stand alone, requiring a connector piece or a bit of joinery.

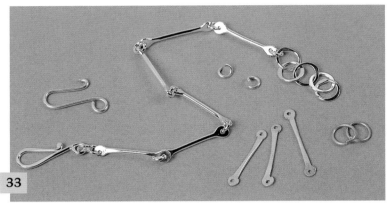

The basic components of most chains are (from left to right): an S hook, clasp circles, links, and connector circles.

Joinery

Connector circles are small circles that discretely join two links. I've made the ones in this book a standard size: 18-gauge wire wrapped over a needle file handle, unless otherwise indicated. Allow 1/2 inch (1.3 cm) of wire for each standard connector circle. These are about as small as you can get. Certainly you could use larger ones; they're more noticeable and can function as design elements, such as in the Oval Stack chain on page 82.

Of course, to be a wearable piece of art, the ends of a chain have to fasten together. Any kind of clasp or hook can be used. Check with suppliers for prefabricated closures such as a toggle or spring-loaded lobster clasp. The project chains use a stylized, handmade S hook that's similar in design to those available from a jewelry supply source. The next section tells you how to make a nice one.

In certain designs, the S hook slips into one of a series of *clasp circles* at the chain's end. Such a closure will let you adjust the chain's length to the size of your neck or to complement a clothing neckline. Unless otherwise noted, standard clasp circles are made from 18-gauge wire wrapped over a 1/4-inch-diameter (6 mm) mandrel; allow 1 inch (2.5 cm) for each one. Other designs don't need clasp circles because the hook can be inserted into any point or link along the chain.

Making an S Hook

I like to use a nice, flowing S hook for all my clasps. It's easy to make and far superior to a purchased finding, because its surface, finish, and proportions are perfectly matched to the rest of the chain.

Photo 34 on page 39 shows the shaping stages of making an S hook. To begin, bend a small or medium side loop at one filed end of a

2-inch (5 cm) piece of 16-gauge wire. This is where the chain will be attached later, so leave the joint unsoldered. At the other end, bend a half loop. With the base of the round nose pliers, bring the half loop around to meet the joint of the side loop (see photo 35).

The projects will tell you when a different gauge

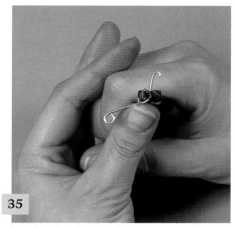

34

The stages of making an S hook: a straight wire is bent into a side loop at one end and a half loop at the other before the piece is fashioned into an asymmetrical U shape.

35

The last bend of an S hook

wire or length of wire should be used for the hook, but all are made the same way despite changes in gauge or length. To make the clasping action smoother, ball the half loop.

Making Lengths of Chain

Each of the project instructions provides the measurement for a single link. You may wonder why. Well, making chain the right length requires a bit more planning than, say, stringing beads.

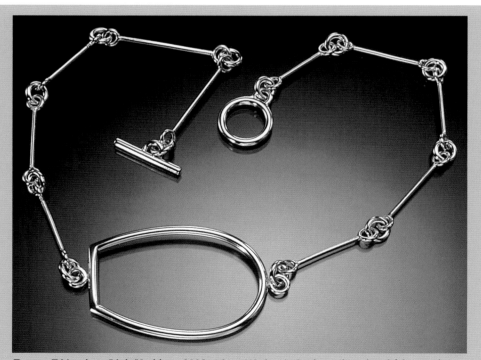

Donna D'Aquino, *Link Necklace,* 2003. 16 in. (40.6 cm). Sterling silver; hand fabricated.
Photo by Ralph Gabriner

You'll find that it's far more efficient—and you'll achieve greater consistency from link to link—if you know how many links you need before you start. Make them all before moving on to the next stage of the process.

First, determine the length of the finished chain. Next, subtract from that number the lengths of the hook (1 inch [2.5 cm]) and clasp circles, if they're used (also 1 inch [2.5 cm]). Finally, divide the link measurement into the remaining chain length. If connector circles are in the design, I've incorporated them into the measurement of the length of the link. To figure out the number of connector circles needed, count the number of links and add 2 to that number.

For example, with a 20-inch (50.8 cm) chain with hook and clasp circles, one link and connector circle might measure $1/2$ inch (1.3 cm). You'd need to make 36 links and 38 connector circles.

To simplify matters, you'll probably want to make your finished pieces to standard lengths in bracelets (7 to 8 inches [17.8 to 20.3 cm]), ankle chains (9 to 11 inches [22.9 to 27.9 cm]), and necklaces (15 inches [38.1 cm] or more). And made longer still, a chain can even fit a waist!

More Jewelry for Your Time

As long as you're making links, consider that earrings are easily created from the individual links of a chain and are a great way to emphasize that the link is itself a design piece. Most designs require nothing more than a way to fasten the link to the ear lobe. They can dangle on an ear wire or use a post, clip-on, or screw-back attachment. A post requires an earring nut to keep the short piece of wire in the ear. The clip-on or screw-back styles are more complex to make and often better purchased from suppliers (photo 35). These two types of attachments often require redesigning the links or other special considerations. The ear wire, also known as a French wire, is the easiest attachment to make for an earring and, of the three designs, arguably the most secure. If you'd rather not make them, all findings are available through suppliers.

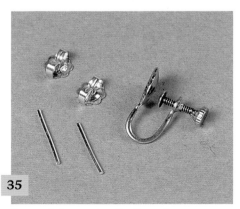

35

Some of the earring findings that are available from suppliers

Making Ear Wires

You'll need 2¼ inches (5.7 cm) of 20-gauge sterling silver wire. Make a small ball at the burred end of the wire. File the other end until it's smooth, and lightly polish it for comfortable wear. With round nose pliers, make a small side loop. That's where you'll attach the link of the chain. Using a ¼-inch (6 mm) mandrel, bend the wire away from the side loop. Now there's the necessary space for the earlobe. At the straight end of the wire, bend a small angle so the wire will slip into an ear comfortably (see photo 36).

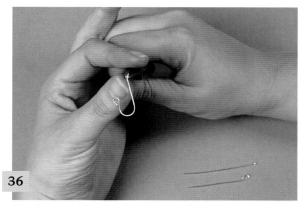

36

The last stage in shaping an ear wire

Only when you pick up the tools can you bring to life the processes I've demonstrated here. Play with the tools and materials to get a better feel for them. Do the quick technique warm-ups before moving on to the projects. The projects are organized to move you along gently, so start with the very first one. You will probably find yourself referring back to informational sections in moments of frustration or confusion. At those times, take a break and return to face the challenge with a relaxed mindset. Even to this day, I make myself walk away from projects that don't seem to be working and return later to realize the solution with a clearer mind. During those challenging moments you'll learn more than any book could ever teach, and you'll learn a lot about yourself. So jump into the projects, but give yourself time to understand.

Andrea L. McLester, *Merchant of Venice,* 2004.
20 in. (50.8 cm). Sterling silver, flame-worked glass. Photo by artist

Design

A chain is dynamic. In essence, it is a miniature kinetic sculpture, so its design should be intentional, relying on basic design elements to create a three-dimensional art form that's exciting to wear and beautiful to look at.

Subtle elements of a chain affect the "feel" of a design, whether it's organic or geometric, industrial or feminine. These qualities are expressed in the weight and thickness of the wire, its texture, the shapes and sizes of the links, and whether they're ornate or plain. I recommend playing with the materials to discover new ways of working the wire and to find other ways of expressing your intention.

To simplify the creation process and your understanding of chain making, the project chains shown in this book use link designs that are mostly two-dimensional (i.e., they have height and length but lie more or less flat against the skin). As you gain confidence in the design arena, consider emphasizing the third dimension, and when you find the right way to do something, write it down. It will help you replicate the process later.

Design Elements

There are many subtle qualities in a design that affect the way it looks to the human eye. Jewelers use these design elements to make their work both appealing and functional.

Form is the shape and contour of an object in both static and dynamic styles. For example, the basic link might look like a recognizable object, such as in the Baseball chain (page 80), or have a more abstract form, like the Amoeba chain (page 56).

Space refers to the visual and physical area that the design assumes. Some chains lie flat while others project into space; some

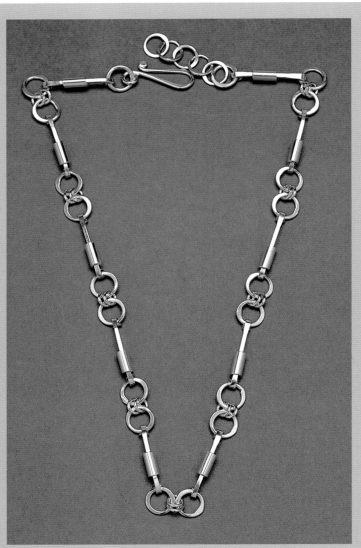

Chantal Saunders, *Sliding Tube,* 1999. 16 in. (40.6 cm). Sterling silver wire and tubing; hand fabricated, forged. Photo by Stewart O'Shields

are solid metal forms, and others are more open, like filigree. A chain has a visual line along which our eyes travel, though the individual links also express linear qualities; these might be straight and angular, or curvy and flowing. Texture is visual as well as tactile. Hammered textures can be smooth or bumpy, and nearly anything else in between, and these may be natural—sometimes called "organic"—or industrial. Almost any object that can make a mark on metal can be used to texture it.

The effect of light on a chain's reflective surface is entirely dependent on its shape, space, line, texture, and environment. Even color from skin tone, hair, and clothing subtly change the perceived design. Using only one color of metal in a chain gives it unity and focuses the eye on shape. And the metal's native color has its own subjective qualities: silver is a "cooler" color than gold, and copper feels warmer still than gold. Silver has great whitish color. Later, you might try using more than one kind of metal in your own designs to achieve unusual effects.

Movement is the flexibility with which the joinery moves, altering the way the chain looks or feels. A chain might be rigidly designed so that the movement of the wearer doesn't affect the look of the chain; other designs may flow freely, so even subtle motion constantly changes the look of the piece.

A chain that's made from a single material, such as silver wire, puts the emphasis on the shape of the link's basic form and economizes its design. If stones or other embellishments are added to links, those become the focal point and alter the emphasis of the overall design. Start simple and you'll learn fast.

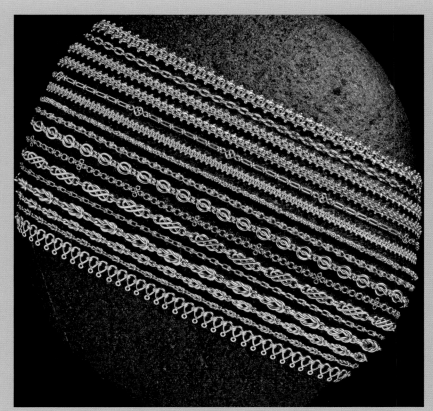

Lucie Heskett-Brem, *Gold Weaver Collection,* 1988–1991. Various lengths. 20-karat yellow gold, 20-karat red gold; handmade. Photo by Louis Brem

Quick sketches for jewelry designs

Design Principles

In addition to the basic elements of design that are part of every creative process, chains must be functional and wearable and also acknowledge such real-world qualities as weight, strength, and the physics of joinery.

Gravity

Even after it's constructed and assembled, the most beautiful chain of your imagination will take on a life of its own. All chains are

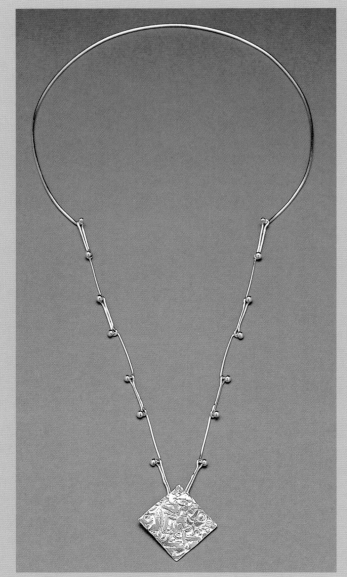

Chantal Saunders, *Triangulation,* **2002. 22 in. (55.9 cm).**
Sterling silver; fused, hand fabricated. Photo by Stewart O'Shields

affected by gravity, and a good design considers this fact to attain a particular look and movement in the chain. Every chain has a central balance point, or axis, from which two links pivot. This is always the widest part of the open space in a link. For instance, a chain of squares ends up looking like a chain of diamonds because the widest part of a square link is from one diagonal corner to the other. The natural axis of a link can be altered by specifying a different pivot point, or by limiting its range of movement.

When the chain is worn on the body, gravity changes things even more. Around the neck, the heaviest part of the chain naturally finds its way to the chest and is very visible. Around the wrist, the heaviest part of a chain falls to the inside of the wrist and is hidden. Adding a few heavy rings, for extra weight, or using lighter materials in certain sections, to reduce weight, can help solve many gravity-based problems.

If you learn to anticipate the effects of gravity on your design you won't be surprised or disappointed by the final look of the chain when you wear it.

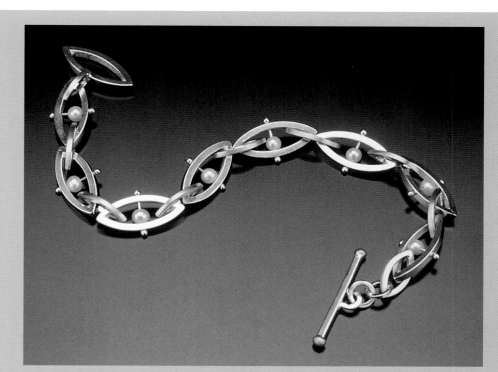

Danielle Miller-Gilliam, *Marquise Bracelet,* 2003. 7½ in. (19 cm). Sterling silver, 18-karat gold, pearls; hand fabricated, cast. Photo by Tim Barnwell

Body

All sculpture must have a setting, and a chain's setting is on the body. Naturally, a chain should be limited in size and weight to what an average person can wear. And it should be comfortable to wear; a barbed-wire chain might look beautiful but unless its sharp edges are rounded, it won't be suitable to wear. Outside its typical setting it can be an amazing piece of art, but for a chain's design to be successful, it must be useful.

Longevity

All chains should be strong enough to withstand a little abuse, ensuring years of wearing adornment. There are simple ways to add strength when it's needed. The first rule of thumb: The larger the span of the openness in the design, the heavier the wire gauge needed to increase its strength. Unsoldered links usually require this solution. Second, links with solder joints are stronger than wire links alone. Soldering loops, circles, or the free end of a piece of wire easily adds strength so that lighter, more delicate-looking designs are just as durable as heavier ones.

Joinery

For the projects in this book, you'll be joining links to form lengths of chains in many ways. The projects use connector circles, pins, loops, and sometimes the links themselves to connect the chain, and how they work together affects the final flow and look of the design. For example, the links in the Wiggle chain lie flat while the connector circles are in opposition to them, but each Amoeba link lies perpendicular to its neighbor. When designing a chain, remember that each successive connection will be perpendicular to the last. There are many other forms of joinery, too. Rivets, hinges, or any permanent mechanical means for creating a pivot point will result in a flexible piece that can then be joined with others to create a chain. Understanding the range of flexibility in a joint will allow you to control how tightly or loosely the chain moves.

Now that you have a basic knowledge of the tools, materials, and principles essential to chain design and chain making, you're ready to begin your own chain making adventure. The last rule of thumb…always have fun!

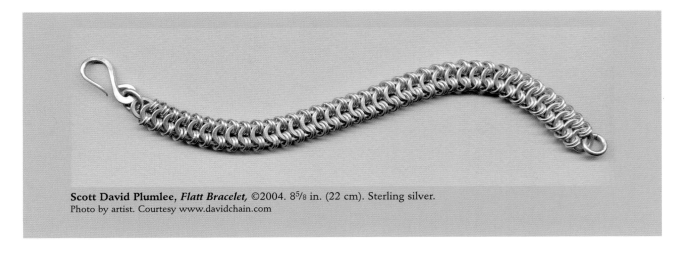

Scott David Plumlee, *Flatt Bracelet,* ©2004. 8⅝ in. (22 cm). Sterling silver.
Photo by artist. Courtesy www.davidchain.com

Danielle Miller-Gilliam, *Bubbles Necklace,* 2004. Adjustable, 16 or 18 in. (40.6 or 45.7 cm). Sterling silver, 18-karat gold, 14-karat gold, blue topaz, amethyst, peridot; hand fabricated, forged. Photo by Robert Diamante

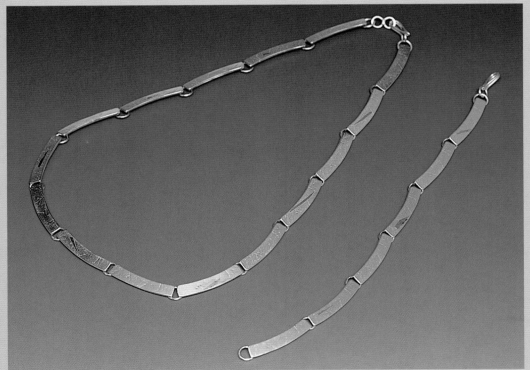

Above: Ellen Vontillius, Untitled, 2000. 16 in. (40.6 cm). Sterling silver, London blue topaz; hand fabricated, cast. Photo by Randall Smith

Left: Sadie Wang, *Textured Series: Long Curved Rectangular,* 2001. Necklace, 15¹⁄₅ in. (39.4 cm); bracelet, 6¹⁄₂ in. (16.5 cm). Photo by R.H. Hensleigh

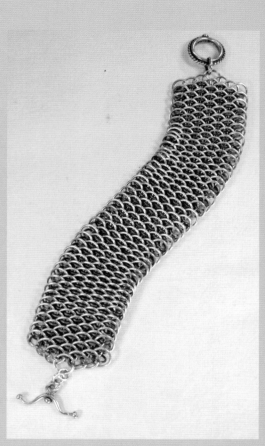

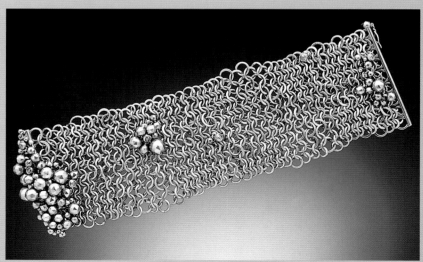

Above: Anne E. Mitchell, *Mermaid's Mesh,* 2002. 22½ in. (55.9 cm). Sterling silver; oxidized. Photo by Steven Nersesian

Top right: Robert Ebendorf, *Bracelet,* 2004. 8 in. (20.3 cm). Mixed media, found parts. Photo by Bobby Hansson

Center right: Patty L. Cokus, *Salt to Taste,* 1999. 8 in. (20.3 cm). Hand blown glass, salt inclusions, copper, sterling silver, patina; blown directly into hand-fabricated frames, oxidized. Photo by Dean Powell

Right: Lola Brooks, *Bracelet,* 2003. 7½ in. (19 cm). Stainless steel, rose-cut diamonds, 18-karat gold; hand fabricated. Photo by Dean Powell

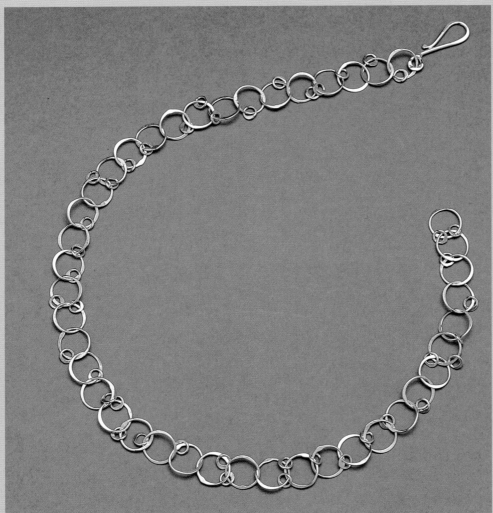

Lynda Watson, *Megan's Birthday—Salt Spring Island,* 2001. 6¾ in. (17 cm). Dine silver, sterling silver, pencil drawing on paper, watch crystal, stones with barnacles; hand fabricated, oxidized. Photo by Hap Sakwa

Left: Chantal Saunders, *Orbit,* 2000. 16 in. (40.6 cm). Sterling silver; hand fabricated, forged. Photo by Stewart O'Shields

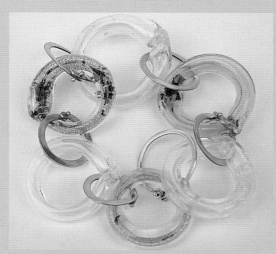

Patty L. Cokus, *Season,* 2003. (19 cm). Hand blown glass, salt inclusions, pepper inclusions, 14-karat yellow gold. Photo by Dean Powell

Kristin Diener, *Salt Reliquary: Fork,* 2004. 8 in. (20.3 cm). Sterling silver, drapery hardware, button holders; hand fabricated. Photo by Margot Geist

Kristin Diener, *Travel Lust Reliquary: Places I've Lived and Favorite Locations,* 2001. 21 in. (53.3 cm). Sterling silver, gold, watch crystals, road atlas, model car tires, mica, teeth, bone, gunshells, bottle caps, pearls, found objects; hand fabricated. Photo by Pat Berrett

51

Left: Kathleen Lynagh House,
Rectangle Bracelet, 2004. 8 in. (20.3 cm). Sterling silver; cast, hand assembled, soldered, polished. Photo by Hap Sakwa

Below: Josephine Jacobsmeyer, Untitled, 2003. 22 in. (55.9 cm). Sterling silver, amber; hand fabricated. Photo by Don Casper, Casper Photoworks

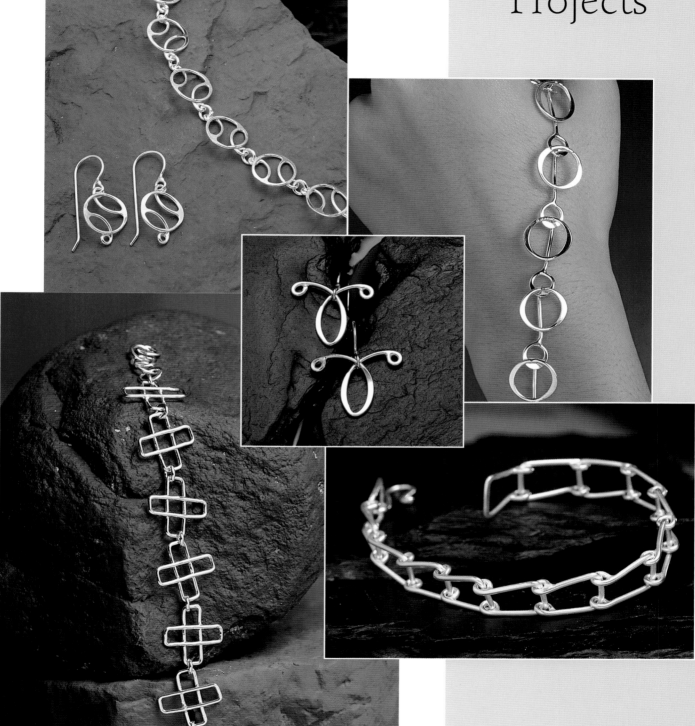

Circle

This bold, classic piece uses simple design elements and introduces you to the basics of chain making.

Tools and Materials

For a necklace 16 inches (40.6 cm) long

16-gauge sterling silver wire, 51 inches (129.5 cm) long

16-gauge sterling silver wire, 2 inches (5.1 cm) long, for the hook

Mandrel, 1/2 inch (1.3 cm) in diameter

File

Planishing hammer and block

Chain nose pliers

Note: 1 link measures 5/8 inch (1.6 cm)

Instructions

1 Wrap and cut 26 circles on the mandrel. File the ends.

2 Link together all the circles and lay them on the soldering block (see photo 1). Rotate the joints so you have clear access to them for soldering. Flux and solder each circle closed. Pickle and rinse.

3 Make a standard S hook and link it to the chain. Flux and solder the link closed; pickle and rinse.

4 Spot forge the hook and two opposing areas on each circle.

5 Tumble the chain in stainless steel shot for 8 hours.

Earring Variation: *To make matching earrings, attach a pair of linked circles to each ear wire.*

1

Amoeba

Fashioning the whimsical freeform links in this piece will acquaint you with shaping wire.

Note: 1 link measures 1 inch (2.5 cm)

Tools and Materials

For a necklace 18 inches (45.7 cm) long

18-gauge sterling silver wire, 51 inches (129.5 cm) long

16-gauge sterling silver wire, 2 inches (5.1 cm) long, for the hook

Mandrel, ³⁄4 inch (1.9 cm) in diameter

File

Round nose pliers

Half round–nose pliers

Chain nose pliers

Forging hammer and block

Instructions

1 Wrap and cut 17 circles on the mandrel. File the ends.

2 Link together all the circles, lay them on the soldering block, and rotate the joints so they're accessible for soldering. Flux and solder. Pickle and rinse.

3 Make a standard S hook and link it to the chain. Flux and solder the link closed. Pickle and rinse.

4 Using the different pliers, randomly shape each circle to create amoebic shapes (see photo 1). You can emulate the forms shown in the photo, or make up your own. There's no right or wrong way to shape the links, but too many bends and kinks can make the chain look busy.

5 Spot forge the hook, and forge each amoebic shape in no more than four spots. Don't overdo it, however, because 18-gauge wire is thin.

6 Tumble in stainless steel shot for 8 hours.

Earring Variation: *Make matching earrings by attaching a single shaped link to each ear wire.*

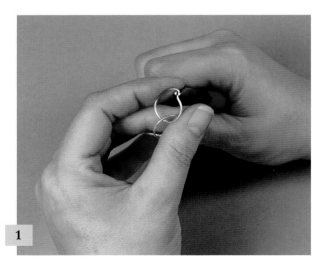

1

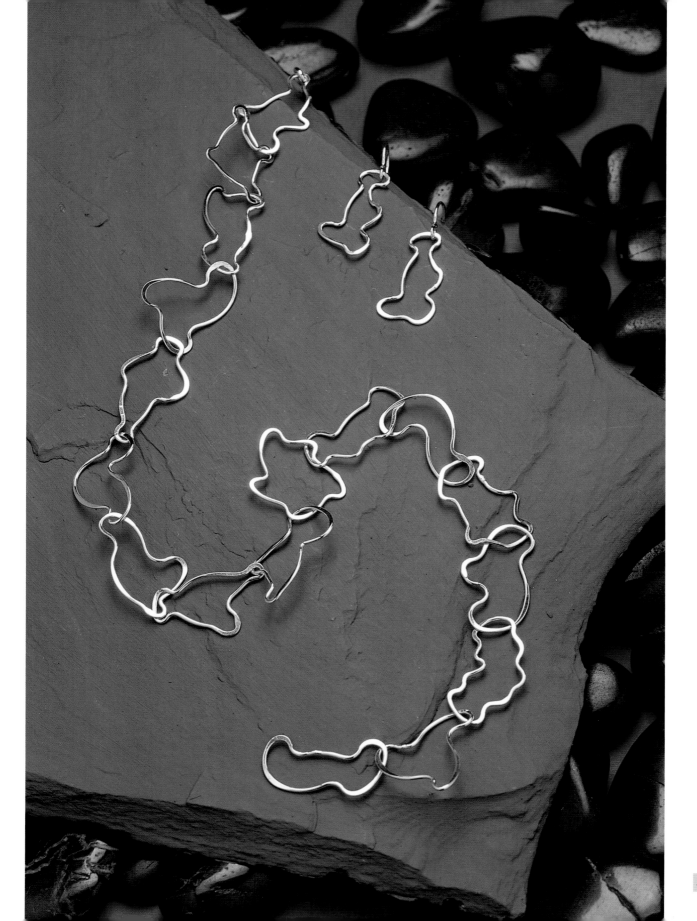

Geometric

A handmade quality is still evident in the clean, strong shapes of this bracelet. Making it will hone your soldering skills and refine your wire shaping skills.

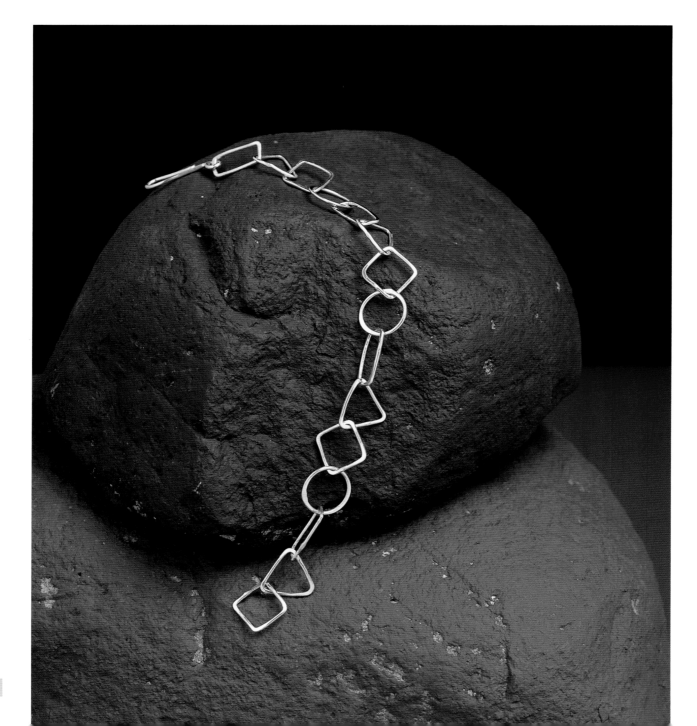

Tools and Materials

For a bracelet 8 inches (20.3 cm) long

18-gauge sterling silver wire,
23 inches (58.4 cm) in length

16-gauge sterling silver wire,
2 inches (5.1 cm) long,
for the hook

Mandrel, 3/8 inch (1 cm)
in diameter

File

Flat nose pliers

Chain nose pliers

Forging hammer and block

Note: 1 link measures 1/2 inch (1.3 cm)

Instructions

1 Wrap and cut 15 circles.
File the ends.

2 Link together all the circles
and lay them on the soldering block. Rotate the joints so
they're accessible for soldering.
Flux and solder each circle. Pickle
and rinse.

3 Make a standard S hook,
and link it to the chain.
Flux and solder the hook closed.
Pickle and rinse.

4 Using both of the pliers,
fashion the circles into geometric shapes, alternating the
forms as you go. Don't forget to
leave a few circles round! Start
with a loose version of the shape,
then make the contours tighter
and sharper by pulling the corners into the edge of the pliers
while pushing the wire against
the pliers (see photo 1). To avoid
making trapezoids, fashion the
angles carefully and keep the
opposite sides of the squares or
rectangles the same length.

5 Forge the hook and the
corners of each geometric
shape. Forge the circles in two
spots.

6 Tumble in stainless steel
shot for 8 hours.

Earring Variation: *Fashion
matching earrings by attaching a
pair of shaped links to each ear wire.*

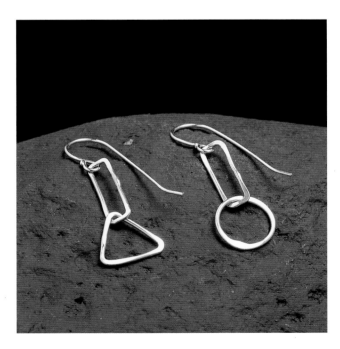

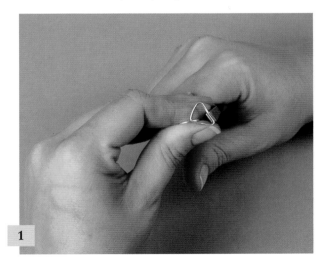

1

Spine

The rhythmic flow of this design's links creates a striking overall effect. When you create this chain, you'll learn how to make and solder loops.

Note: 1 link measures ¹³/₁₆ inch (2.1 cm)

Tools and Materials

For a necklace 16 inches (40.6 cm) long

18-gauge sterling silver wire, 34 inches (86.4 cm) in length

16-gauge sterling silver wire, 2 inches (5.1 cm) long, for the hook

18-gauge sterling silver wire, enough for 5 clasp circles

File

Round nose pliers

Chain nose pliers

Forging hammer and block

Instructions

1 Mark and cut 18 pieces of wire, each 1½ inches (3.8 cm) long. File the ends.

2 On each piece, form a straight loop with the small end of the round nose pliers. Place all the pieces on the soldering block, then flux and solder the straight loops closed. Pickle and rinse.

3 On each piece, use the base of the jaw of the round nose pliers to form a side loop at a 90-degree angle, perpendicular to the straight loop.

4 Use the chain nose pliers to open the larger loop, and attach a link (see photo 1). Continue to add links, making sure they all face in the same direction. Complete the length of chain.

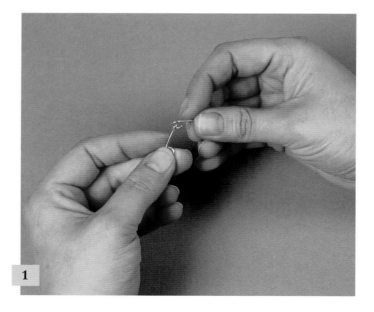

1

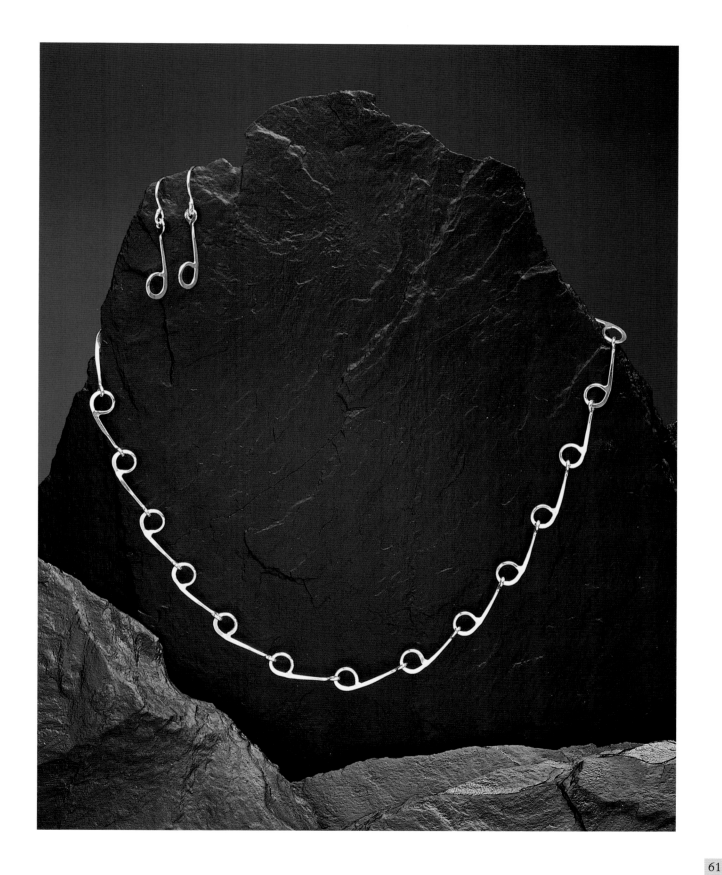

Spine

5 Place the chain on the soldering block so that each solder joint faces you. Flux the chain and solder each joint. Pickle and rinse.

6 Make an S hook 1³/₄ inches (4.4 cm) long. Make 5 clasp circles. File their ends, if necessary. Attach the hook, put the end links in place, and solder. Pickle and rinse.

7 Forge each large loop, then forge the straight part of each link (see photo 2). It's easier to forge small sections of chain on the block rather than maneuver the links to complete all the hammering at once. Forge the hook and the end links.

8 Tumble in stainless steel shot for 8 hours.

Earring Variation: *Matching earrings are made by fashioning two elements. Follow the instructions through step 3, forge each element as in step 7, then attach one to each ear wire.*

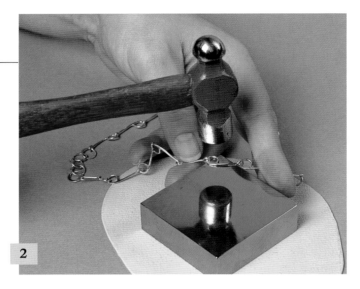

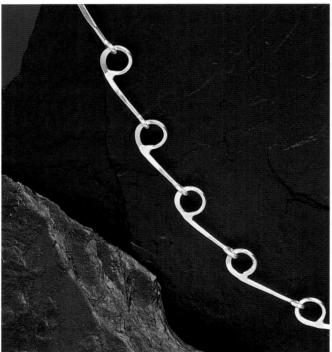

Wiggle

Once you've made this softly flowing chain you'll be familiar with how to ball wire and solder connector circles.

Wiggle

Note: 1 link measures 1⅛ inches (2.9 cm)

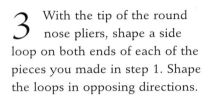

Tools and Materials

For a necklace 16 inches (40.6 cm) long

16-gauge sterling silver wire, 26 inches (66 cm) long

16-gauge sterling silver wire, 2 inches (5.1 cm) long, for the hook

18-gauge sterling silver wire, enough for 5 clasp circles and 14 connector circles

Round nose pliers

Chain nose pliers

Instructions

1 Mark and cut 12 pieces of wire, each 2 inches (5.1 cm) long. Make round balls at both ends of each piece. Pickle and rinse.

2 While the pickle does its job, make the hook, 5 clasp circles, and 14 connector circles that will be used later in the project.

3 With the tip of the round nose pliers, shape a side loop on both ends of each of the pieces you made in step 1. Shape the loops in opposing directions.

4 Using the round nose pliers, hold a link in the middle of the straight part of the wire (see photo 1, on page 65). Create a slight S shape by holding the balled side in your fingers and slightly twisting the pliers in the opposite direction (see photo 2). Shape each link in the same way, repeating the same direction of twist for each.

5 Place the links on the soldering block. Flux the links and solder each loop closed. Pickle and rinse.

6 Use the chain nose pliers to join the links with the connector circles so that the direction of the S curves remains consistent along the chain. Add connector circles to the ends of the length of chain. Rotate the connector circles so that each joint is accessible, then flux and solder them closed. Pickle and rinse.

7 Attach the hook and clasp circles, flux, and solder. Pickle and rinse.

8 Tumble in stainless steel shot for 8 hours.

Earring Variation: *Create matching earrings by making 2 links, following the shaping instructions, and attaching each to an ear wire.*

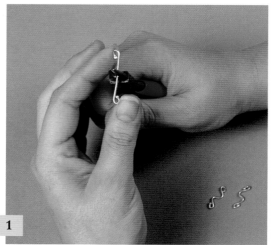

1

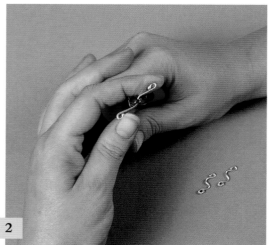

2

Bar

Making this spare and modern chain design will help you get the knack of drilling holes and forging wire balls.

Tools and Materials

For a bracelet 8 inches (20.3 cm) long

14-gauge sterling silver wire, 7½ inches (19 cm) long

16-gauge sterling silver wire, 2 inches (5.1 cm) long, for the hook

18-gauge wire, enough for 5 clasp circles and 8 connector circles

Forging hammer and block

File

16-gauge (1.3 mm) twist drill bit

Needle file

Chain nose pliers

Note: 1 link measures 1 inch (2.5 cm)

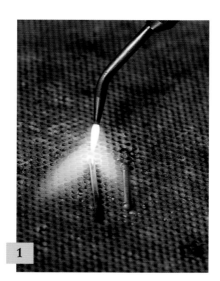

1

Instructions

1 Mark and cut 6 pieces of wire, each 1¼ inches (3.2 cm) long (see photo 1). Make flat balls at both ends of each piece. Pickle and rinse.

2 While waiting for the pickle to accomplish its job, make the S hook, 5 clasp circles, and 8 connector circles to use later in the project.

3 Forge each balled end of the pieces from step 1 so they're flat. Work slowly and lightly, because hard and fast hammer blows will cause cracks in the balls. Lightly file and polish the edges of the forged balls, if necessary.

4 Drill a hole in each flattened ball. Be sure not to drill too close to the edge or it will weaken the joint. Remove any metal burrs with a needle file. Polish any scratched links, if necessary.

5 Using chain nose pliers, join all the links of the chain with connector circles. Add connector circles to the ends of the length of chain. Place the chain on the soldering block. Rotate the connector circles into view, then flux and solder them closed. Pickle and rinse.

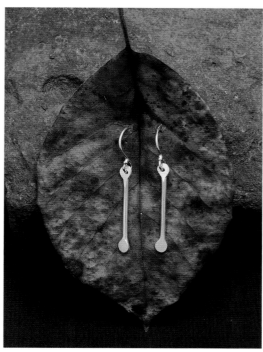

6 Attach the hook and clasp circles, then flux and solder them closed. Pickle and rinse.

7 Forge the hook and clasp circles.

8 Tumble in stainless steel shot for 8 hours.

Earring Variation: *For matching earrings, cut 2 wires. Shape and forge the links as described, but drill a hole in only 1 end of each wire. Link a bar to each ear wire.*

Scallop

Pin connections are a novel way to keep the focus on the links' shapes. Here's a versatile design that's elegant enough for evening wear.

Tools and Materials

For a necklace 16 inches (40.6 cm) long

16-gauge sterling silver wire, 20 inches (50.8 cm) long

20-gauge sterling silver wire, 10 inches (25.4 cm) long

16-gauge sterling silver wire, 2 inches (5.1 cm) long, for the hook

18-gauge sterling silver wire, enough for 5 clasp circles

Mandrel, 1/2 inch (1.3 cm) in diameter

Forging hammer and block

File

.84- to .90-mm twist drill bit

Needle file

Cross-locking tweezers

Note: 1 link measures 13/16 inch (2.1 cm)

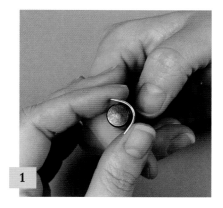

Instructions

1 Mark and cut 18 pieces of the 16-gauge wire, each 1 inch (2.5 cm) long. Bend the wires over the mandrel to form a soft U or scallop shape (see photo 1).

2 Forge both ends of the scallop. Make the hammered ends no larger than 1/8 inch (0.3 cm) wide. File the ends to remove any burrs and round out the shapes.

3 Drill holes in each end of the scallops. File any burrs from the holes. Polish the shapes, if necessary.

4 Mark and cut 18 pieces of the 20-gauge wire, each 1/2 inch (1.3 cm) long. (You might make a few more because they're tiny and easy to lose.) Ball one end of each of the 20-gauge pieces by holding the middle of the wire with the cross-locking tweezers. Melt the metal until the ball meets the tweezers.

5 To assemble the chain, slip a pin into the underside of the hole in one scallop, add another scallop, and melt the top of the pin into a ball (see photo 2). Continue adding pins and links, making sure the curve of the scallops in the assembly remains consistent along its length. Each link in the chain should have the left end of the scallop on top of its neighbor and the right end underneath. (A torch hanger is useful when you're picking up and putting down the torch so often). Once you have joined all the scallops with pins, pickle and rinse the chain. While you're waiting, make the hook and 5 clasp circles.

6 Make two 20-gauge connector circles. Attach them to the ends of the chain. Pickle and rinse.

7 Attach the hook and clasp circles, then flux and solder. Pickle and rinse.

8 Forge the hook and clasp circles.

9 Tumble the necklace in stainless steel shot for 8 hours.

Earring Variation: *Assemble a pair of earrings by cutting 4 pieces of 16-gauge wire and following the instructions through step 3, but drill a hole in only one end of each scallop. Attach pairs of scallops to each ear wire so their curves face each other and they cross at the bottom.*

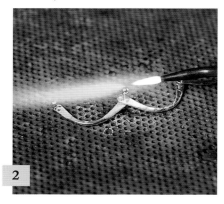

Spiral

Imaginative forging turns ordinary spirals into fanciful links that spring to life in this chain design.

Note: 1 link measures 1 inch (2.5 cm)

Tools and Materials

*For a bracelet 8 inches
   (20.3 cm) long*

18-gauge sterling silver wire,
   39 inches (99.1 cm) long

16-gauge sterling silver wire,
   2 inches (5.1 cm) long,
   for the hook

18-gauge sterling silver wire,
   enough for 5 clasp circles and
   13 connector circles

Mandrel, ½ inch (1.3 cm)
   in diameter

Round nose pliers

Forging hammer and block

Chain nose pliers

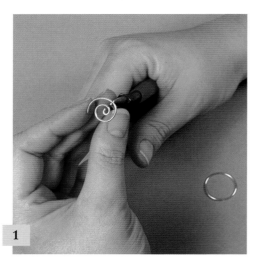

Instructions

1. Wrap and cut 11 circles on the mandrel. Shape the circles into a loose spiral by holding one end of the wire with the round nose pliers and bending the wire toward the inside, using even pressure from your thumb. Move the pliers up along the wire as you curve it into shape (see photo 1).

2. Lay all the spirals on the soldering block facing in the same direction. Make flat balls at both ends of the spirals. Pickle and rinse. While waiting for the pickle to work, make the S hook, 5 clasp circles, and 13 connector circles.

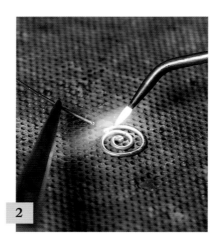

3. Reshape the spiral to achieve its final contour by bending the outer balled end into the side of the spiral. Solder the ball to the wire spiral (see photo 2). Pickle and rinse.

4. Forge each spiral in two opposing areas, being careful not to hit the balls.

5. With chain nose pliers, link together all the spirals with connector circles, joining them so they face the same direction. Add connector circles to the ends of the length of chain.

6. Rotate the joints so they're accessible for soldering. Lay the chain on the soldering block, then flux and solder each connector circle. Pickle and rinse.

7. Link the hook and clasp circles to the chain. Flux and solder. Pickle and rinse.

8. Forge the hook and clasp circles.

9. Tumble in stainless steel shot for 8 hours.

Earring Variation: *It's simple to make matching earrings. Follow the instructions to make 2 spirals, and attach one to each ear wire.*

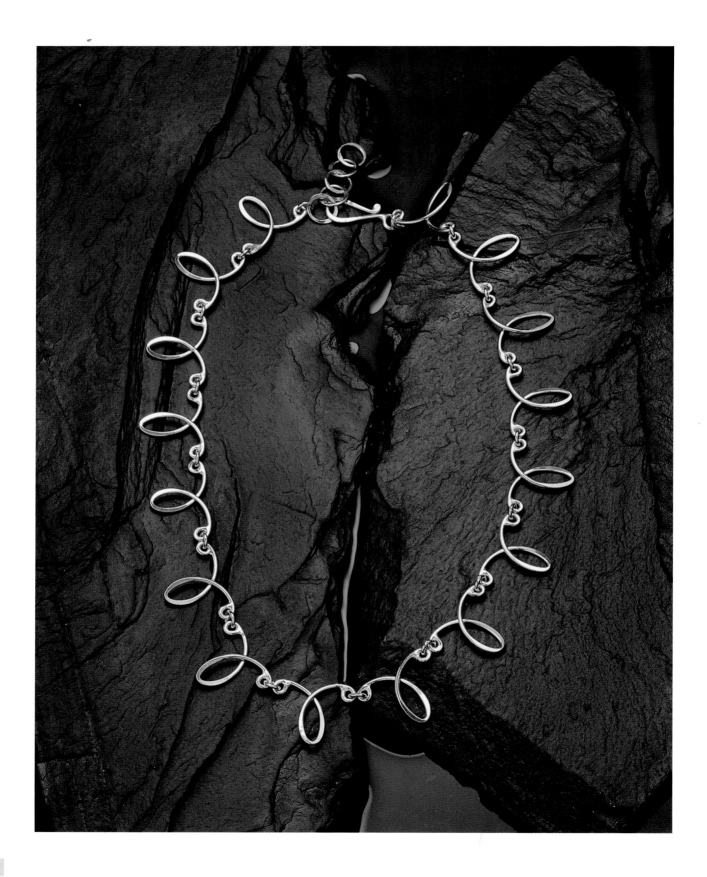

Teardrop

The dramatic flair of this chain design relies on organic link shapes that started as simple open circles.

Note: 1 link measures 7/8 inch (2.2 cm)

Tools and Materials

For a necklace 16 inches (40.6 cm) long

16-gauge sterling silver wire, 44 inches (111.8 cm) long

16-gauge sterling silver wire, 2 inches (5.1 cm) long, for the hook

18-gauge sterling silver wire, enough for 5 clasp circles and 18 connector circles

Mandrel, 3/4 inch (1.9 cm) in diameter

Chain nose pliers

Round nose pliers

Forging hammer and block

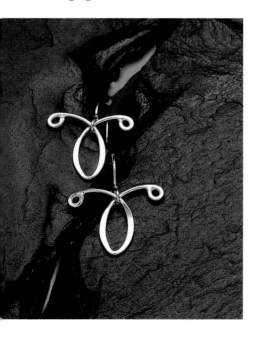

Instructions

1 Wrap and cut 16 circles. With the chain nose pliers, bend each circle at its midpoint so the sides cross each other equally enough to form an oval or teardrop shape between them.

2 Shape side loops at each of the wire's ends with the small tip of the round nose pliers (see photo 1). Flux and solder the side loops closed. Pickle and rinse.

3 Make the hook, 5 clasp circles, and 18 connector circles.

4 Forge each of the teardrop links (see photo 2). Polish them, if necessary.

5 Put the connector circles between the side loops to make the length of chain. Add connector circles to the ends. Rotate the joints so they're accessible for soldering, flux the chain, and solder each connector circle closed. Pickle and rinse.

6 Attach the hook and end links to the chain. Flux and solder. Pickle and rinse.

7 Forge the hook and end links.

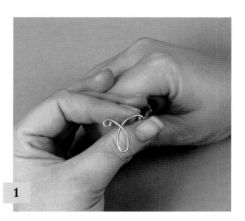

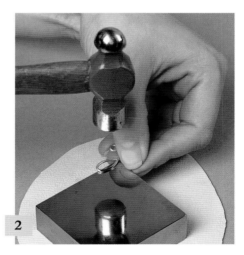

8 Tumble in stainless steel shot for 8 hours.

Earring Variation: *To fashion earrings, make 2 teardrops; the central loops should be a bit larger than those for the chain. Attach each one to an ear wire.*

Tadpole

Nature inspired this lyrical link design to evoke a graceful, organic form. Good sense memory skills will help you get the curls just right.

Tools and Materials

For a necklace 16 inches (40.6 cm) long

18-gauge sterling silver wire, 44 inches (111.8 cm) long

16-gauge sterling silver wire, 2 inches (5.1 cm) long, for the hook

18-gauge sterling silver wire, enough for 5 clasp circles

File

Round nose pliers

Chain nose pliers

Forging hammer and block

Note: 1 link measures ⁷/₈ inch (2.2 cm)

Instructions

1 Mark and cut 18 pieces of wire, each 2 inches (5.1 cm) long. File the ends. Form a side loop on each piece, using the base of the jaw of the round nose pliers. Make three small bends with the tip of the round nose pliers (see photo 1). Use the chain nose pliers to squeeze the bends gently so the wires meet. Bend the remaining wire so that it comes straight out of the tadpole-shaped part.

2 Place each piece on the soldering block. Flux and solder the large loops. Pickle and rinse.

3 While waiting, make an S hook and 5 clasp circles.

4 Forge the exterior curves of each completed tadpole shape. With the round nose pliers, make a medium-size side loop at the straight end of each wire that is perpendicular to the other loop.

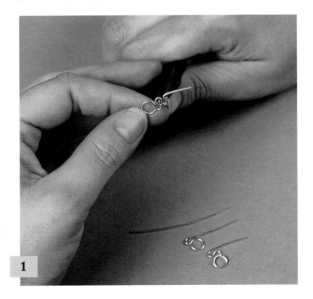

1

Tadpole

5 Using the chain nose pliers, open the medium loop sideways and attach the large loop of another link. Make sure that all the links are attached in the same direction. Complete the length of the chain.

6 Place the chain on the soldering block so that the medium loop stands straight up off the block (see photo 2). Flux the chain and solder each medium loop joint. Pickle and rinse.

7 Attach the hook and clasp circles. Flux and solder them closed. Pickle and rinse.

8 Forge the hook and clasp circles.

9 Tumble in stainless steel shot for 8 hours.

Earring Variation: *To make matching earrings, follow the instructions to make 2 tadpole shapes, and attach each by the small loop to ear wires.*

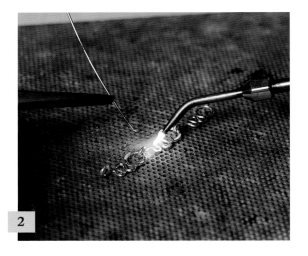

2

Demi-Circle

This demi-circle chain cleverly tricks the eye. Paired links like these offer great design possibilities.

Demi-Circle

Note: 1 link measures ⁷/₈ inch (2.2 cm)

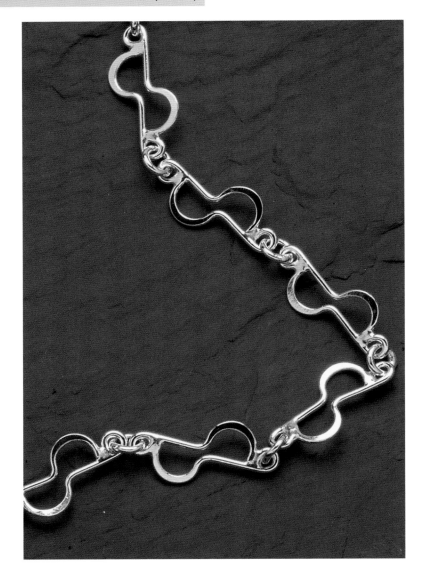

Tools and Materials

For a bracelet 8 inches (20.3 cm) long

18-gauge sterling silver wire, 18 inches (45.7 cm) long

16-gauge sterling silver wire, 2 inches (5.1 cm) long, for the hook

18-gauge sterling silver wire, enough for 5 clasp circles and 9 connector circles

File

Round nose pliers

Forging hammer and block

Chain nose pliers

Instructions

1 Mark and cut 14 pieces of wire, each 1 inch (2.5 cm) long. File the ends. On one end of each wire, make a small side loop. Using the base of the round nosed pliers, bend a straight half loop in the same direction as the side loop (see photo 1).

2 Arrange two pieces opposite each other so that the end of the half loop of one piece meets the inside of the small side loop of the other. There should be a gap at the center of the shape. If necessary, reshape the pieces so they fit.

3 Place a pair on the soldering block, making certain to check the shape, then flux and solder the small loop and the end of the half loop together (see photo 2). If they are touching, everything will solder at the same time. Repeat for all the links. Pickle and rinse.

4 While waiting, make the S hook, 5 clasp circles, and 9 connector circles.

5 Forge each of the demi-circle links on both sides of the outer part of the half circle.

6 Using chain nose pliers, join the links with connector circles, making sure that all the links face in the same direction. Add connector circles to the ends of the length of chain.

7 Place the chain on the soldering block, rotating the joints so they're accessible. Flux and solder the connector circles closed. Pickle and rinse.

8 Attach the hook and clasp circles, then flux and solder. Pickle and rinse.

9 Forge the hook and clasp circles.

10 Tumble in stainless steel shot for 8 hours.

Earring Variation: *For a pair of earrings, cut 4 pieces of wire and follow the instructions in steps 1 through 3 to make 2 links. Forge them as directed in step 5, then attach each one to an ear wire.*

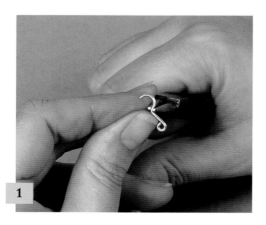

1

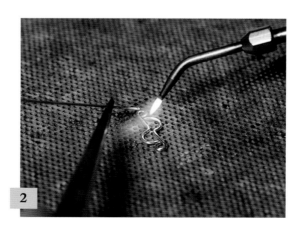

2

Baseball

This symmetrical design, made by joining two simple elements, evokes a familiar sports theme.

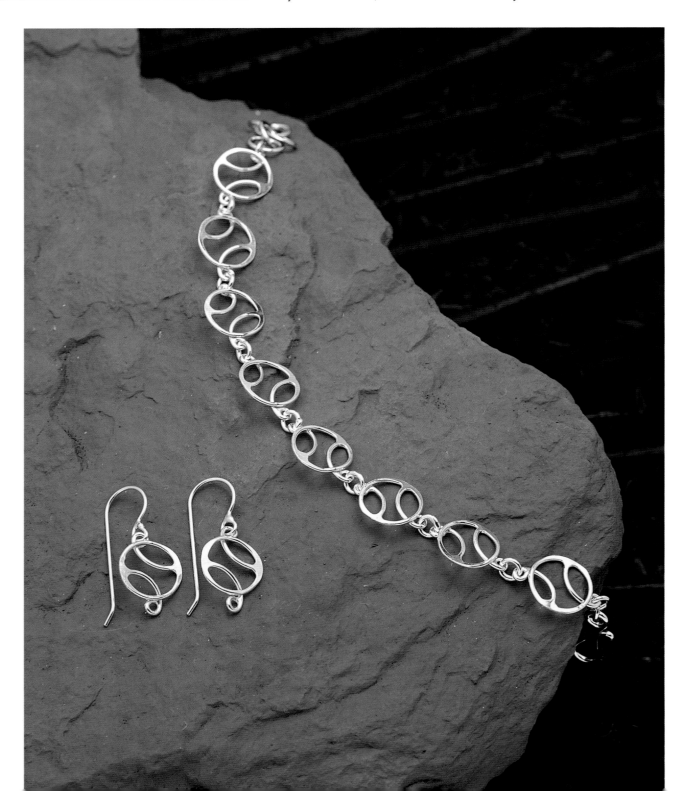

Tools and Materials

For a bracelet 8 inches (20.3 cm) long

18-gauge sterling silver wire, 28 inches (71.1 cm) long

16-gauge sterling silver wire, 2 inches (5.1 cm) long, for the hook

18-gauge sterling silver wire, enough for 5 clasp circles and 10 connector circles

Mandrel, 3/8 inch (1 cm) in diameter

Chain nose pliers

Round nose pliers

Forging hammer and block

File

Note: 1 link measures 13/16 inch (2.1 cm)

Instructions

1 Wrap and cut 16 circles. Shape the circles with the chain nose pliers by first finding the midpoint of the circle. Bend the circle at this point so the sides cross each other equally to form an oval shape with legs (see photo 1).

2 Use the round nose pliers to shape a small side loop on only 1 leg of each oval. Be sure to make the side loop on the same side. Solder the side loops closed. Pickle and rinse.

3 While the pickle works, make the S hook, clasp circles, and 10 connector circles.

4 Arrange the shaped links in pairs on the soldering block so they from a baseball shape, aligning the links so that the circular outline is nicely rounded. Flux and solder both joints of each baseball link (see photo 2). Pickle and rinse.

5 Forge each link on both sides of the solder joint. File the shape to round its edge, and polish it.

6 Join each link with the connector circles to make the length of chain. Add connector circles to the ends of the length of chain. Rotate the joints so they're accessible for soldering. Flux the chain and solder each connector circle. Pickle and rinse.

7 Link the hook and clasp circles to the chain. Flux and solder. Pickle and rinse.

8 Forge the hook and end links.

9 Tumble in stainless steel shot for 8 hours.

Earring Variation: *Follow the directions to make 2 links, and attach each by a loop to an ear wire.*

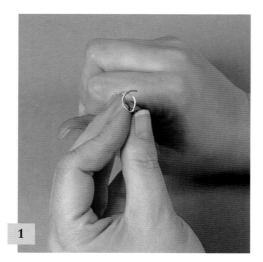

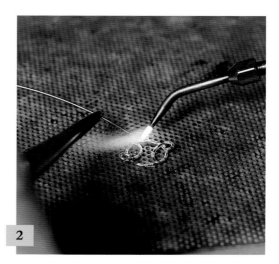

Oval Stack

Hammered textures and strong graphic shapes enliven this chain design.

Note: 1 link measures 1⅛ inches (2.8 cm)

Tools and Materials

For a necklace 17 inches (43.2 cm) long

16-gauge sterling silver wire, 112 inches (284.5 cm) long

16-gauge sterling silver wire, 2 inches (5.1 cm) long, for the hook

18-gauge sterling silver wire, enough for 41 clasp circles

Mandrel, ½ inch (1.3 cm) in diameter

File

Round nose pliers

Riveting and forging hammers and block

Instructions

1 Wrap and cut 39 circles. File the ends. Align all the circles closed and place them on the soldering block so the joints are free. Flux and solder each joint. Pickle and rinse.

2 Slip each circle over the closed jaws of the round nose pliers, and open the tool to stretch the circle into an oval, making sure the solder joint is not on the jaw of the pliers (see photo 1). The joint should be on a side of the oval and not in a bend. Pull hard to make the sides flat.

3 Arrange the ovals side by side in groups of three. Flux and solder the sides of the stacked ovals to attach them together. Pickle and rinse.

4 Make an S hook. Make 41 clasp circles and reserve 36 of them to use as large connectors.

5 File and polish the soldered ovals, if necessary. Forge the outer curves flat. With a riveting hammer, lightly texture both sides of the straight portions (see photo 2). Flip over each piece and ham-

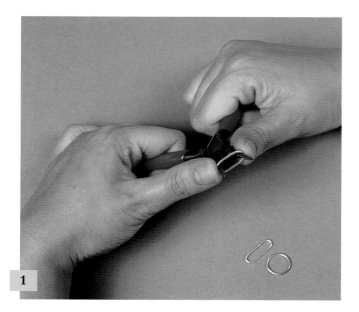
1

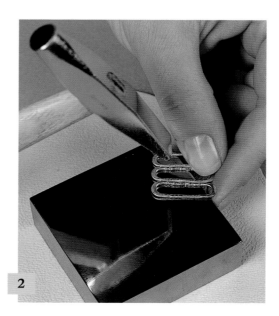
2

Oval Stack

mer it lightly. Be careful; if you hammer too hard, the blows will cause the texture on the other side to flatten out.

6 Join the stacked ovals by linking them with connectors only in the top and bottom ovals. Add the remaining connectors to the ends of the length of chain. Lay out the chain with the joints rotated into view, then flux and solder the connectors closed. Pickle and rinse.

7 Join the end connectors together with another connector to form a triangular group of links (see photo 3). Attach the hook and clasp circles to the ends. Flux and solder all the remaining circles. Pickle and rinse.

3

8 Spot forge the connectors, clasp circles, and hook.

9 Tumble in stainless steel shot for 8 hours.

Earring Variation: *For matching earrings, cut 6 wires. Follow the instructions in steps 1 through 3 to fashion 2 sets of stacked ovals, and forge them as directed in step 5. Make a ¼-inch (0.6 cm) connector circle, cut it in half, and file the ends. Solder a half circle to each of the oval stacks, in the center of a flat area. Attach each stack to an ear wire.*

Joined Snakes

This light, streamlined chain needs fewer links because each one is a bit longer than is traditional. This project is great practice for making wire balls and developing your hammering technique.

Joined Snakes

Note: 1 link measures 1⁵/₁₆ inches (3.4 cm)

Tools and Materials

For a bracelet 8 inches (40.6 cm) long

14-gauge sterling silver wire, 13¹/₂ inches (39.4 cm) long

16-gauge sterling silver wire, enough for 5 clasp circles

File

Round nose pliers

Chain nose pliers

Forging and riveting hammers and block

Instructions

1 Mark and cut 5 pieces of 14-gauge wire, each 2¹/₄ inches (5.7 cm) long. File only one end of each wire. With the round nose pliers, shape a small side loop at the filed end. Shape the rest of the wire with soft rolling bends that end in a straight bit of wire centered over the loop.

2 Using the chain nose pliers, bend a neck ¹/₈ to ¹/₄ inch (0.3 to 0.6 cm) long into the last bit of wire so it looks stepped from the side (see photo 1). Try to make each piece 1¹/₄ inches (3.2 cm) long from the tip of the loop to the location of the bend. This will help create the pin joint later.

3 Place the "snakes" on the soldering block. Flux and solder the side loops closed. Pickle and rinse.

4 Meanwhile, make a 2¹/₄-inch (5.7 cm) S hook from the 14-gauge wire; it should have a smaller side loop and longer legs than a standard hook. Also, make 5 standard clasp circles with the 16-gauge wire.

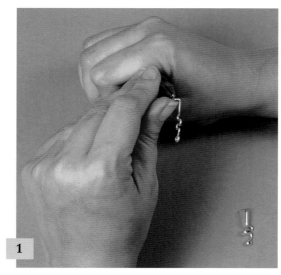

1

5 Polish the snakes, if needed. To give them texture, forge down the top of each link with a riveting hammer (see photo 2).

6 To join the links, slide the neck of one snake into the side loop of another, checking that the correct side is face up. Slide the link down to the loop end. Turn the link upside down, flux the wire, and melt an upside-down flat ball on the end of the snake to create a pin joint (see photo 3). The ball should melt to meet the neck. Repeat with the other links. Pickle and rinse.

7 Attach the clasp circles to the loop end of the chain. Open the hook's side loop and wrap it around the pin joint of the other end of the chain. The circle should be smaller than the ball of the pin joint. Flux and solder the hook and clasp circles closed. Pickle and rinse.

8 Forge the clasp circles and hook. Forge the head of the snake links flat. Gently bend each link to create a soft hump so the bracelet will fit smoothly over a wrist.

9 Tumble the chain in stainless steel shot for 8 hours.

Earring Variation: *The ear dangles are made from 2 wires. Follow steps 1 through 3 to make the "snakes," forge them, and attach each looped end to the ear wires. Forge the free ends flat.*

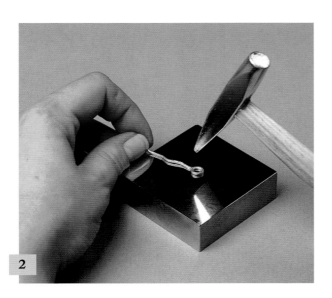

2

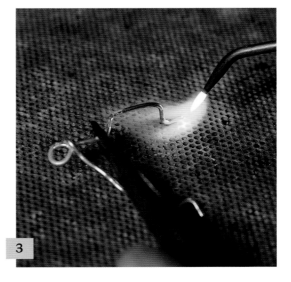

3

Square Cross

This light, modern chain design creates an entirely new form from a single design element.

Note: 1 link measures $^7/_8$ inch (2.2 cm)

Tools and Materials

For a bracelet 8 inches (20.3 cm) long

16-gauge sterling silver wire, 38 inches (96.5 cm) long

16-gauge sterling silver wire, 2 inches (5.1 cm) long, for the hook

18-gauge sterling silver wire, enough for 5 clasp circles and 9 connector circles

Mandrel, $^1/_2$ inch (1.3 cm) in diameter

File

Round nose pliers

Chain nose pliers

Forging hammer and block

Instructions

1 Wrap and cut 14 circles. File the ends. Align all the circles closed. Place them on the soldering block so the joints are accessible. Flux and solder each one. Pickle and rinse.

2 Slip each circle over the closed jaws of the round nose pliers, making sure the solder joint isn't on the jaw of the tool. Open the pliers to stretch the circle out into an oval, pulling hard to get the sides flat. When all the circles are stretched, form the round ends into a squared rectangular shape with chain nose pliers (see photo 1).

3 Lay one rectangle over another to make a square cross. Flux and solder the spots where the wires cross, directing the flame at the bottom rectangle (see photo 2). Pickle and rinse.

4 While waiting, make an S hook, 5 clasp circles, and 9 connector circles.

5 Polish the square crosses, if necessary. Join pairs of them together with a connector

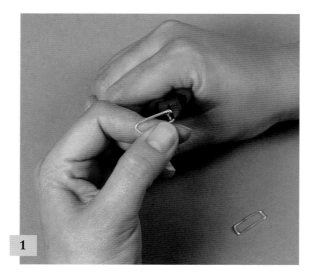

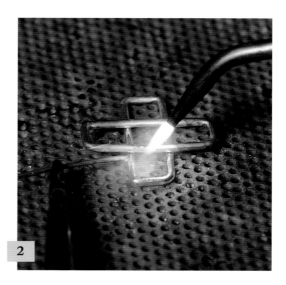

Square Cross

circle. Add connector circles to the ends of the length of chain.

6 Place the chain on a soldering block, rotating the joints so they're accessible. Flux and solder the connector circles closed. Pickle and rinse.

7 Attach the hook and clasp circles to the ends of the chain, then flux and solder them closed. Pickle and rinse.

8 Forge the clasp circles and hook.

9 Tumble in stainless steel shot for 8 hours.

Earring Variation: *For the earrings, follow steps 1 through 3 to make 2 square crosses. Make a connector circle, cut it in half, and file the ends. Solder a half circle to both square crosses. Use this loop to attach each element to an ear wire.*

Paddle

One ingenious wire shape forms both the link and the pin-style connection. The result is a sinuous, light chain.

Paddle

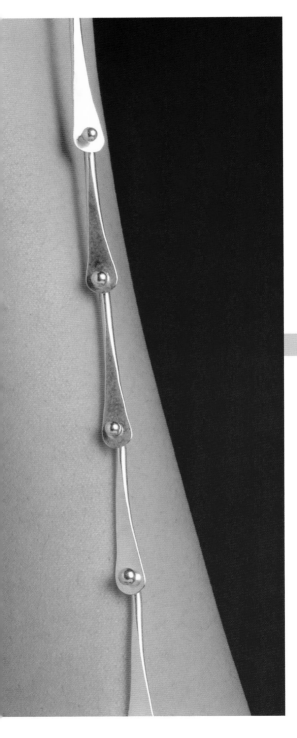

Tools and Materials

For a necklace 16 inches
(40.6 cm) long

14-gauge sterling silver wire,
19½ inches (49.5 cm) long

14-gauge sterling silver wire,
enough for an S hook

16-gauge sterling silver wire,
enough for 5 clasp circles

Chain nose pliers

Flat file

1.7-mm twist drill bit

Needle file

Forging hammer and block

Note: 1 link measures ⁷/₈ inch (2.2 cm)

Instructions

1 Mark and cut 17 pieces of wire, each 1 inch (2.5 cm) long. With the chain nose pliers, bend one end of each piece 90 degrees to form a ¼-inch (0.6 cm) pin.

2 On the other end of the wire, hammer out a paddle shape no wider than ³/₁₆ inch (0.5 cm), as shown in photo 1. File the ends until they're nicely round.

3 Drill a hole in each paddle, centering it a minimum of ⅛ inch (0.3 cm) from the edges. De-burr the drilled holes with a needle file and polish any marred links.

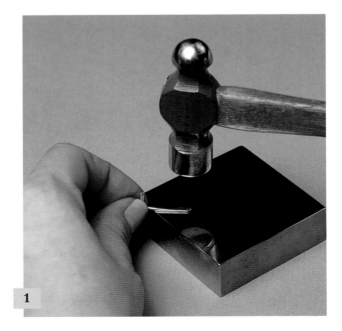

1

4 Place the links on the soldering block, joining one link to another with the pins facing up. Flux the links. Use a horizontal flame to melt the end of each wire until a ball forms (see photo 2). Make sure the ball is large enough so it won't slip out of the drilled hole, but be careful not to melt the thin end of the other paddle. Complete the length of chain. Pickle and rinse.

5 Make an S hook with a small loop from the 14-gauge wire and 5 clasp circles from the 16-gauge wire. Note that these are made from slightly heavier wire than is recommended for most of the other projects in this book.

6 Once the chain is pickled, attach the hook to the ball end of the last link. Attach the clasp circles to the end with the drilled hole. Flux and solder the hook and clasp circles closed. Pickle and rinse.

7 Forge the clasp circles and hook.

8 Tumble in stainless steel shot for 8 hours.

Earring Variation: *To make earrings, use 2 wires, and follow steps 1 and 2. Make a ball at the unforged ends of both wires. Shape front-facing loops on each ear wire, and attach the paddle links to them. Affix the links to ear wires.*

2

Square Scale

Square links are rather unusual. This design's motif is open and airy, yet it makes for a chain with great presence.

Tools and Materials

For a bracelet 8 inches (20.3 cm) long

16-gauge sterling silver wire, 29 inches (73.6 cm) long

16-gauge sterling silver wire, 2 inches (5.1 cm) long, for the hook

File

Flat nose pliers

Round nose pliers

Mandrel, ³/8 inch (1 cm) in diameter

Forging hammer and block

Note: 1 link measures ¹/2 inch (1.3 cm)

Instructions

1 Mark and cut 13 pieces of wire, each 2 inches (5.1 cm) long. File the burred ends. With flat nose pliers, shape each wire into a squared U shape, making sure that all the legs of the Us are of equal length.

2 With round nose pliers, make small 90-degree side loops on both ends of each wire, making sure they're all positioned on the same side (see photo 1). Polish any links, if necessary.

3 Use the flat nose pliers to open the side loops sideways, just wide enough to slip them onto the square end of the next link. Align the side loops closed. Repeat to complete the chain.

4 Lay the chain on the soldering block so that the side loop joints are facing up. Flux the chain and solder each joint closed. In doing so, point the flame straight down a short distance away from the joint, to ensure the end doesn't melt (see photo 2). Pickle and rinse.

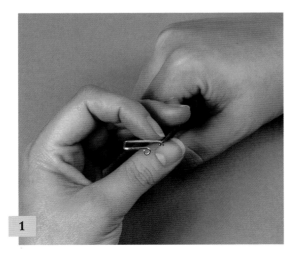

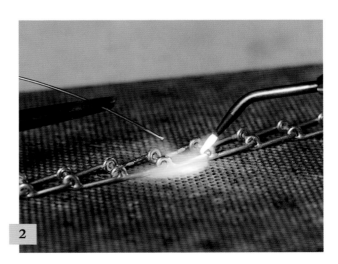

5 Make an S hook and, using the mandrel, one 16-gauge circle.

6 Join the circle to both side loops at the last link on the chain. Attach the hook to the other end. Flux and solder these in place. Pickle and rinse.

7 Shape the circle into a square as you did in step 1. Hammer the last square links on both ends of the chain to allow the hook to slide on easily.

8 Tumble in light to moderately abrasive medium for 8 hours.

Earring Variation: *To make a pair of earrings, you'll first shape a triangular loop on each ear wire. Starting with 4 pieces of wire, follow steps 1 through 4 to make 2 sets of 2 links each, and attach 1 to the triangle on each ear wire.*

Butterfly

Each link is a detailed and festive wire drawing, and such a design is just the thing to test your wire-bending and soldering skills.

Butterfly

Tools and Materials

*For a bracelet 8 inches
  (20.3 cm) long*

18-gauge sterling silver wire,
  41 inches (104.1 cm) long

16-gauge sterling silver wire,
  2 inches (5.1 cm) long,
  for the hook

18-gauge sterling silver wire,
  enough for 5 clasp circles and 8
  connector circles

Mandrel, 3/4 inch (1.9 cm) in
  diameter

Chain nose pliers

Round nose pliers

Half round pliers

Forging hammer and block

Note: 1 link measures 1/2 inch (1.3 cm)

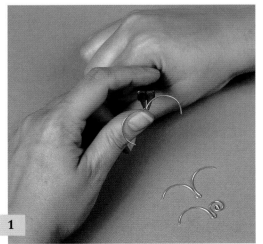

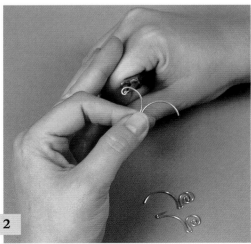

Instructions

1 Wrap and cut 12 circles. Bend each circle in half with the chain nose pliers so that it's fully opened into a double U (see photo 1).

2 Using the round nose pliers, shape one end of each piece into a spiral that follows the curves of the form (see photo 2). At the other end, use the chain nose pliers to bend a 1/4-inch (0.6 cm) "antenna" going in the direction opposite the spiral (see photo 3). With the half round pliers, shape the antenna side of each wire to form a smaller circle or oval. This makes one half of a butterfly link.

3 Lay the half-links in pairs on the soldering block so that they form complete butterfly shapes. You may need to make slight adjustments in their shapes so that the antennae and spiral ends touch each other. Flux and solder each butterfly at those points. Pickle and rinse.

4 Reshape each butterfly so that the midpoints meet and the tips of the antennae don't touch anything else. Lay them out on the soldering block, and flux and solder the midpoint joint. Flip over the butterflies and lightly melt the spiral and antenna ends into flat balls (see photo 4). Pickle and rinse.

5 While waiting, make an S hook, clasp circles, and 8 connector circles.

6 With a hammer and block, forge the butterfly shapes lightly in five spots—once on the antennae, and on the outer curves of each wing. Be sure to hit the balls for added sparkle. Polish where necessary.

7 Join the wings of the butterflies with connector circles. Add connector circles to the ends of the length of chain. Rotate the joints for easy access, and flux and solder the connector circles closed. Pickle and rinse.

8 Attach a hook and clasp circles to the ends. Flux and solder the hook and clasp circles. Pickle and rinse.

9 Forge the hook and clasp circles.

10 Tumble in stainless steel shot for 8 hours.

Earring Variation: *A pair of earrings will require 2 ear wires and 2 butterfly links. Follow steps 1 through 4, and then 6, to fabricate and forge the butterflies. Fashion a large loop on each ear wire, then solder the butterfly onto the ear wire.*

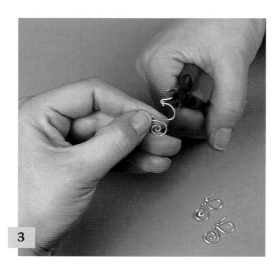

3

4

Layered Circles

There's strength in numbers, and this chain proves it. It utilizes a more delicate 20-gauge wire and complex soldering patterns that will challenge your skills.

Tools and Materials

*For a bracelet 8 inches
(20.3 cm) long*

20-gauge sterling silver wire,
98 inches (248.9 cm) long

16-gauge sterling silver wire,
2 inches (5.1 cm) long,
for the hook

18-gauge sterling silver wire,
enough for 6 standard
clasp circles

Mandrel, 3/8 inch (1 cm) in
diameter

File

Forging hammer and block

Note: 1 link measures 7/16 inch (1.1 cm)

Instructions

1 Wrap and cut 65 circles. File the ends. Align the ends of 35 of the circles so they're closed. Arrange the 35 closed circles on the soldering block, then flux and solder each one closed. Pickle and rinse. Leave the remaining 30 circles open.

2 At the soldering station, arrange the 30 open circles in six groups of 5 circles each. Divide the 35 soldered circles into four groups, three with 10 circles each, and the last with 5 circles.

3 Join 5 open circles, 1 at a time, with a group of 10 soldered circles. After you align each open circle's ends, flux and solder it closed (see photo 1). Repeat for the other two groups of 10 soldered circles. Pickle and rinse. You'll now have three short sections of layered chain, a group of 5 soldered circles, and three groups of 5 open circles.

4 Divide the group of 10 links in a short section in half. Make sure none of the links crosses or twists.

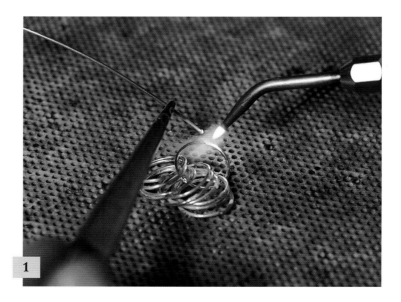

1

Layered Circles

5 Use 5 open circles, 1 at a time, to join the last 5 unlinked soldered circles to one of the 5-ring groups you made in step 4 (see photo 2), fluxing and soldering each as you go. Pickle and rinse.

6 Use another group of 5 open circles, 1 at time, to join the remaining short sections of chain to each other, making sure that you work with only the 5 end circles on each section. Flux and solder as usual, and pickle and rinse once you're done. You now have two sections of layered chain, and a group of 5 open circles left.

7 Join the ends of the two sections with the last 5 open circles, fluxing and soldering them one at a time. Pickle and rinse.

8 While waiting, make an S hook and 6 clasp circles.

9 Forge each soldered circle on the chain in two spots (see photo 3).

10 Attach a clasp circle to an end of the chain, and attach the hook to that. Attach five joined clasp circles to the other end. Flux and solder them closed; pickle and rinse.

11 Forge the hook and clasp circles.

12 Tumble in stainless steel shot for 8 hours.

Earring Variation: *To make a pair of earrings, wrap and cut 20 circles. For each earring, align and solder 5 circles, then join 5 open circles to them, one at a time. After you align each open circle's ends, flux and solder it closed. Fashion an extra-large loop on each ear wire, to which you'll attach a section of 5 closed circles from each short length of chain.*

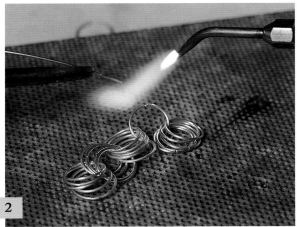

2

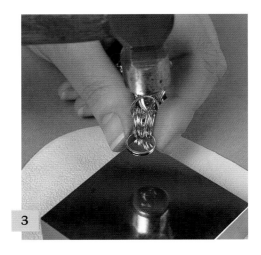

3

Bubble

These simple circles stand away from the body, giving the piece a more dimensional aspect than most chains.

Bubble

Tools and Materials

For a bracelet 8 inches (20.3 cm) long

16-gauge sterling silver wire, 20 inches (50.8 cm) long

16-gauge sterling silver wire, 2 inches (5.1 cm) long, for the hook

18-gauge sterling silver wire, enough for 5 clasp circles

Mandrel, 3/8 inch (1 cm) in diameter

File

Round nose pliers

Forging hammer and block

Chain nose pliers

Instructions

1 Mark and cut 6 pieces of wire, each 1½ inches (3.8 cm) long. Using the rest of the wire, wrap and cut 6 circles. File all the ends.

2 Using the round nose pliers, make a large straight loop at the end of each straight wire. Align each circle so it's closed. Flux and solder each joint closed, applying more solder than required to the circles. Pickle and rinse.

3 Forge each circle in two places, leaving the solder joints unhammered, and forge the end of the straight loop. With the chain nose pliers, put a ¼-inch (0.6 cm) 90-degree bend at the end of the wires with loops (see photo 1).

4 Lay out the circles on the soldering block. Thread the bent end of a wire into the straight loop of another; push the straight loop all the way down, away from the bend. Turn it upside down and rest the bent end on the excess solder of a circle. Orient it so that the straight wire crosses the diameter of the circle (see photo 2 on page 105). Flux, then heat, until the solder flows and joins the wire to the circle. Repeat the

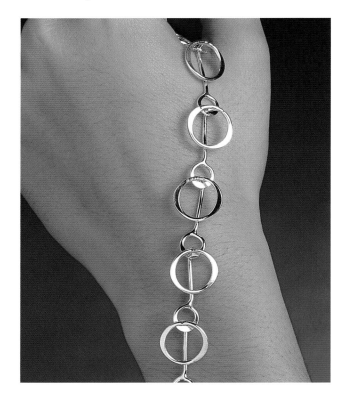

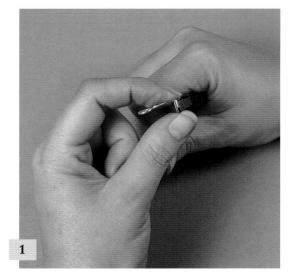

1

threading and joining process until the chain is complete. Pickle and rinse.

5 Make an S hook and 5 clasp circles. Attach the hook to the end of the chain with a large circle, and attach the clasp circles to the end with the straight loop. Arrange the ends on the soldering block; flux and solder. Pickle and rinse.

6 Forge the hook and clasp circles. With light pressure from your thumb, gently curve the straight-wire section of the link. Curve each piece in the same way. The longer the length of chain, the less curvature each link will require. Polish the solder joint of the circle by hand, if required.

7 Tumble in stainless steel shot for 8 hours.

Earring Variation: *For earrings, mark and cut 2 wires, and make 2 circles. Follow the instructions in steps 2 through 4 to make 2 unlinked elements. Forge them as directed, and then attach each to an ear wire.*

Note: 1 link measures ⁷/₈ inch (2.2 cm)

2

Key to Wire Gauges

The projects in this book were made using wire manufactured in the United States, whose standards for wire diameters differ from those in the British system. AWG is the acronym for Brown & Sharpe, or American, wire gauge sizes and their equivalent rounded metric measurements. SWG is the acronym for the Imperial, or British Standard, system in the U.K. Refer to the chart below if you use SWG wire. Only part of the full range of wire gauges that are available from jewelry suppliers is included here.

AWG in.	AWG mm	Gauge	SWG in.	SWG mm
0.204	5.18	4	0.232	5.89
0.182	4.62	5	0.212	5.38
0.162	4.12	6	0.192	4.88
0.144	3.66	7	0.176	4.47
0.129	3.28	8	0.160	4.06
0.114	2.90	9	0.144	3.66
0.102	2.59	10	0.128	3.25
0.091	2.31	11	0.116	2.95
0.081	2.06	12	0.104	2.64
0.072	1.83	13	0.092	2.34
0.064	1.63	14	0.080	2.03
0.057	1.45	15	0.072	1.83
0.051	1.30	16	0.064	1.63
0.045	1.14	17	0.056	1.42
0.040	1.02	18	0.048	1.22
0.036	0.914	19	0.040	1.02
0.032	0.813	20	0.036	0.914
0.029	0.737	21	0.032	0.813
0.025	0.635	22	0.028	0.711
0.023	0.584	23	0.024	0.610
0.020	0.508	24	0.022	0.559
0.018	0.457	25	0.020	0.508
0.016	0.406	26	0.018	0.457

Gallery Contributors

Lola Brooks
New York, New York
Page 49

Patty L. Cokus
Alfred, New York
Pages 49, 51

Donna D'Aquino
Toledo, Ohio
Page 39

Kristin Diener
Albuquerque, New Mexico
Page 51

Robert Ebendorf
Greenville, North Carolina
Page 49

Joanna Gollberg
Asheville, North Carolina
Pages 10, 35

Lucie Heskett-Brem
Meggen, Switzerland
Page 43

Kathleen Lynagh House
La Jolla, California
Pages 27, 52

Josephine Jacobsmeyer
Labadie, Missouri
Pages 23, 52

Hadar Jacobson
Berkley, California
Pages 9, 21

Kristin Lora
Santa Fe, New Mexico
Pages 15, 36

Holly Masterson
Santa Fe, New Mexico
Pages 20, 28

Andrea L. McLester
Rockport, Texas
Page 41

Danielle Miller-Gilliam
Greenville, South Carolina
Pages 13, 45, 47

Anne E. Mitchell
San Francisco, California
Page 49

Scott David Plumlee
Manhattan, Kansas
Page 46

Chantal Saunders
Asheville, North Carolina
Pages 6, 42, 44, 50

Ellen Vontillius
Tampa, Florida
Pages 32, 48

Sadie Wang
Silver Point, Tennessee
Pages 16, 18, 48

Lynda Watson
Santa Cruz, California
Page 50

About the Artist

Chantal Saunders was born in Montreal, Canada, in 1972, and immigrated to North Carolina in 1981. She studied sculpture before becoming a certified welder and pipe fitter in 1994. After a two-year stint as an apprentice with two Chapel Hill–area jewelers, Chantal moved to Asheville to start her own jewelry studio. She's a member of the North Carolina Society of Goldsmiths, teaches chain making workshops, and maintains a website at http://www.metalsplendor.com.

Glossary

area polish—Metal polishing that is confined to specific areas of a piece rather than the overall polishing that is obtained with a tumbler

clasp circle—A small, open wire form; a series of these are used at one end of a chain to hold a hook at the other end

connector circle—A plain, open wire form used to join two links of a chain

connector pin—A small rod, balled at both ends, that provides joinery for links

dead soft—Very malleable; said of fully annealed metal

fire scale—The oxidization of copper in an alloy of sterling silver; brought on by heating the metal, as when soldering it

flat ball—A ball that is created when the end of a wire is melted on a flat surface

flexible shaft—A variable-speed tool with a long arm that holds a drill bit or one of various polishing accessories

flux—The chemical that degreases metal and prepares its surface for solder

forging—Striking metal with a hammer

gauge—A standard scale of the diameter of wire; gauge standards vary in different countries

mandrel—A metal bar around which metal wire is wrapped

media—Small pieces of abrasive or polishing material, whether ceramic or plastic, that are used in a tumbler to polish metal

oxidize—The process whereby oxygen combines with a metal

pickle—An acid solution used to remove the oxidization from metal

round ball—A ball created when the end of a freestanding wire is melted

S hook—A simple, curving closure for a chain

sense memory—The memory of muscular and physical senses

shear—Tearing of metal

shot—Small pellets of stainless steel used in tumbling

side loop—An off-center circle that is shaped at the end of a wire

solder—The process of heating a metal to join it with a metal alloy

spot forge—Changing the shape of a wire in one place with repeated blows of a hammer

straight half loop—A half circle that is shaped, then centered, at the end of a wire

straight loop—A circle that is shaped and centered at the end of a wire

work hardened—Describes metal that has undergone stresses (from shaping or forging) that have caused it to become brittle

Acknowledgments

My gratitude and adulation to Terry Taylor, Suzanne Tourtillott, Kathy Holmes, Stewart O'Shields, and the many others at Lark whose matchless efforts made this book a reality. My appreciation and respect also go to the invaluable teachers and mentors who guided me along the winding path that is refining my art; it would not take up as much room in my heart without you. My love and thanks to those in my life who tolerate and sanction my noisy artistic moods. Merci.

Index